MOVIEBOX

MOVIEBOX

Paolo Mereghetti

Abrams, New York

Text by Paolo Mereghetti, Alessandra Mauro, Franca De Bartolomeis and
Alessia Tagliaventi

Edited by Paolo Mereghetti

Published by arrangement with Agenzia Santachiara

Translated from Italian by Grace Crerar-Bromelow

Original edition copyright © 2012 Contrasto srl, Rome
Photographs copyright © 2012 the photographers
Text copyright © 2012 Paolo Mereghetti
This edition copyright © 2012 Harry N. Abrams, Inc.

Originally published in Italian under the title *Movie:Box* by Contrasto srl, Rome.

Cataloging-in-Publication Data has been applied for and may be obtained from
the Library of Congress.

ISBN: 978-1-4197-0506-9

Printed and bound in China
10 9 8 7 6 5 4 3 2 1

THE ART OF BOOKS SINCE 1949
115 West 18th Street
New York, NY 10011
www.abramsbooks.com

CONTENTS

Marilyn Monroe in *The Misfits*, directed by John Huston, 1960. Photo: Eve Arnold

INTRODUCTION

What is cinema? For a question that has been asked so many times before, what comes to mind is probably one of the very first answers, uttered by the father of the Lumière brothers, who was quite sure that 'cinema was an invention without a future.' But, fortunately, his sons Louis and Auguste were able to show that one should not put too much faith in paternal prognostications.

Lumière's hasty prophecy is in stark contrast to a definition from the director of the beautiful *Finis Terrae* (1929), Jean Epstein: 'Since the sad affair of the Tower of Babel, cinema is the only possible universal language.' This statement, made early in the last century, was about a form of expression (and of art) that was still very new at the time.

The potential of cinema was rapidly realized, as Buster Keaton confirmed when recalling his first encounter with a movie camera when working with Roscoe 'Fatty' Arbuckle. He wrote in *My Wonderful World of Slapstick* (1960): 'Roscoe… took the camera apart for me so I would understand how it worked and what it could do. He showed me how film was developed, cut, and then spliced together. But the greatest thing to me about picturemaking was the way it automatically did away with the physical limitations of the theatre. On the stage, even one as immense as the New York Hippodrome stage, one could only show so much. The camera had no such limitations. The whole world was its stage. If you wanted cities, deserts, the Atlantic Ocean, Persia or the Rocky Mountains for your scenery and background, you merely took your camera to them. In the theatre you had to create an illusion of being on a ship, a railroad train, or an airplane. The camera allowed you to show your audience the real thing: real trains, horses and wagons, snowstorms, floods. Nothing you could stand on, feel, or see was beyond the range of the camera.'

When reading these words and thinking about defining cinema, what is striking is the difficulty of setting limits, of drawing any kind of map. Just when you think you've identified everything, you find that a whole new area of the map has slipped away from you; a new passage opens up sudden and unexpected panoramas. Something that may well have been explored many years ago, but then forgotten completely, is now ready to be decoded and experimented with all over again, like 3D cinema, for instance. Invented in the 1920s, in the time of the Lumière brothers, 3D seemed like the perfect weapon in the battle against the advent of television in the 1950s, and is enjoying a second flourishing today, bringing a new dimension to our vision and entertainment.

In light of this, a book on cinema made up of still photographs might seem a little incongruous. Images printed on paper are fixed and unchangeable, and one might think that they have nothing to do with a world that runs at 24 frames per second, or with the deceptive but undeniable experience of someone who, sitting in a darkened theatre, believes that he or she is watching the reproduction of real life on the screen with all its colour and richness, its excitements and mysteries.

Photography, by its very nature, tends to freeze, stop, transfix. Cinema is fleeting. Or, at least, so it seems, for it takes very

little to set the memory in motion and a single image can be used to recall a whole film. You see a photograph once and you can recall a whole scene, with facial expressions and sounds in the background, and a phrase, a piece of dialogue, will come to mind. It is this strange mechanism that I hope is provoked into action as you leaf through this book, as you are shown what you have already seen, and told something that you already know. When I see a photo of Marilyn Monroe, I think of her playing the ukulele with the other girls in the rhythm section, or of a blast of air from the New York Subway making her skirt fly up around her, or of her appearing out of the Niagara Falls spray wearing a yellow raincoat. Looking at a portrait of Clark Gable, I recall Scarlett O'Hara slapping him, his attempts to hitch a lift with Claudette Colbert, or his rounding up wild horses in the Nevada desert. When I look at a shot of Anna Magnani, I can hear her shouting after the Gestapo jeep that is taking her husband away, I see her again accompanying her daughter to an audition that will change her life, or her welcoming a drifter wearing a snakeskin jacket into her small-town store. Strange indeed, but hardly surprising.

A whole film may be conjured up by a single line: 'After all, tomorrow is another day,' or 'Don't let's ask for the moon. We have the stars,' or, indeed, 'Nobody's perfect.' Those are just a few examples from the thousands that could have been chosen. The magic, complexity, artistry, beauty and sheer entertainment value of films like *Gone with the Wind*, *Now, Voyager* and *Some Like It Hot* are infinitely greater than the witty brevity of these lines. But this is how our recall and pleasure mechanisms work: they need a point of departure, a hook, a stimulus.

And so, when leafing through the following pages, images and memories will become inextricably interwoven, because a portrait will refer to a film, a still from a scene will recall a line, and a web of cross-references and connections will fire the memory and reawaken the imagination. This takes us back to our starting point: what is cinema? Perhaps it is just a state of mind, a pathway between dreams and reality, a way of opening ourselves to experiences hitherto denied to us (but probably all the more

desirable because of this). Journeys are possible that will take us to places we've never been to before, that will create sensations in us which we have never felt before, that will perhaps lead us along highways and byways into a mysterious or secret past. Just as it was for the very first film-goers as they descended into the basement of the Grand Cafè in Paris, to be terrified by a train that seemed to come bursting out of the screen, so it was when *Stagecoach* invited us to climb up onto the driver's seat beside the Ringo Kid on the stage to Lordsburg, which was carrying a pregnant bride, a shy whiskey salesman, a drink-sodden doctor, a hooker with a heart of gold, a gambler and a dishonest banker. And it will be the same for us when we take our seats to follow a spacecraft into the sky, to wait for that passionate kiss, to elude an assassin lying in wait....

It seems that the 'invention without a future' will never come to an end.

Paolo Mereghetti

IN
CLOSE-UP

I have never selected an actor because I was captivated by his cleverness, by his professional skills; just as a lack of experience has never stopped me taking on a non-actor. I look for expressive, characterful faces, which immediately say everything by themselves as soon as they appear on the screen.

Federico Fellini

Al Pacino, 2002. Photo: Bruce Davidson

'**A** portrait! What could be more simple and more complex, more obvious and more profound?' asked French poet Charles Baudelaire as long ago as 1859. Since the invention of photography, portraiture has been one of the principal ways in which it has been used. From the very first daguerreotypes in the late 1830s, the portrait has been charged with preserving the memory of those who are far away, the faces of our nearest and dearest who are no longer with us, and even with being a formal means of recognition, as with the *cartes de visite* so favoured by the middle and upper classes of the period.

Vincent Cassel, 2001. Photo: Fabio Lovino

While Félix Nadar's studio was the destination of choice, where one might have met all sorts of high-ranking people in Paris at the end of the nineteenth century, the more ordinary portraitists also tried hard to include elements of psychological depth, and social symbols, in all their work. 'I have longed unceasingly to make pictures of people…to make likenesses that are biographies, to bring out in each photograph the essential personality that is variously called temperament, soul, humanity.' So said Gertrude Käsebier, an American photographer working at the turn of the twentieth century, when considering how she could continue to make portraits that would, as it were, capture 'the spirit' of her sitters.

Photographing stars, the people we might now call 'celebrities', is a genre within a genre, which has had its own specific evolution, with its own kings and queens, high points and low points. From the 1920s onwards, photographers played a huge part in creating the celebrity system, by bringing us images of movie stars that were like fragments from a wonderful faraway galaxy, inhabited by unapproachable beings, always surrounded by a soft-focus halo that preserved a distance between them and us common mortals. With no television and no social networking sites, the portraits of famous actors had to be clear and easily recognizable and readable. In these photographs, people saw the personifications of gods, captured in images that appeared to reveal everything about them: their perfect features, their excellent postures, their well-proportioned figures and the mysteries that surround all those who, quite simply, live in another dimension.

Shortly before the Second World War, the vast profusion of illustrated magazines and their new readership were demanding more explicit, more moving, more dynamic pictures. Photographers were expected to draw not only on technical, but also on psychological and even gymnastic talents

Simone Signoret, 1952.
Photo: Everett Collection

Humphrey Bogart, 1942.
Photo: Scotty Welbourne

Meryl Streep in *Kramer vs. Kramer*, directed by
Robert Benton, 1979. Photo: Columbia Pictures

to explore and tell us about little-known aspects of the star in front of the lens. In this sense, the master of the psychological portrait was Philippe Halsman, who discarded soft-focus and other effects to seek out the person behind the personality and convinced even some of his most famous subjects to let go of their inhibitions and try taking a liberating leap.

Since then, portraiture has undergone an incredible evolution and whole generations of photographers have created new ways of updating the visual language of the genre and of representing the face, with all its expressiveness and the great range of emotions that it conceals, in unusual and original ways.

In the complex relationship between the photographer and the person being photographed (sometimes a competition, at others a synchronicity), a true ballet is played out in the attempt to catch on film (or on a digital screen) an image that can express a sentiment, or convey character. Both photographer and subject must be able to recognize themselves in the final image.

The mutual trust that arises from working with another person towards the common goal of revealing a personality forces the photographer also to look for

himself in the portraits he creates, as each image is not merely a 'visual story' about a certain person but also, in part, a piece of the photographer's own autobiography.

And now, as we are overwhelmed by floods of images in the media and online, what is it that we look for in a celebrity portrait? Something, perhaps, that can astonish us, surprise us and give us an unstereotyped view. It could be a smile, or even a smirk that shocks us or makes us laugh, but it must be out of the ordinary.

'The point is that you can't get at the thing itself, the real nature of the sitter, by stripping away the surface,' commented Richard Avedon when talking about his portraits. 'The surface is all you've got.'

A.M.

Robert De Niro, 2009. Photo: Francesco Carrozzini

Barbra Streisand, 1965. Photo: Philippe Halsman

Can cinema change a life? For **Martin Scorsese**, the answer is most certainly yes. Growing up on the streets of New York City, where the only choice open to him seemed to be between becoming a gangster or a priest, this son of Italian immigrants found that his love of cinema provided a lifeline; and it also allowed him to focus on his true vocation. At first, this was as an assiduous and ardent film-goer; then as a creative director, whose work is deeply informed by film culture; and now it is also as a benefactor (with his World Cinema Foundation, which every year saves cinematic masterpieces from all periods and countries from oblivion). It is hard to imagine Scorsese ever moving very far from a screen, from a movie camera, or from a cutting table. His work, beginning with his very first short films, has been enriched by the images and inventions of other films and other directors, and this has allowed him to develop his extraordinary capacity for inventing new stories, and new ways of telling them. His inspiration is often realistic, dramatic and blood-soaked: streets like urban jungles, wars between different gangs, conflicts that leave their mark on a life, or the struggle to find one's own place in the world.... But when these stories arrive on the screen, such material immediately appears to be ennobled by Scorsese's delight in storytelling, by his desire to find new, original and thrilling forms. They are never sweetened, but always reinvented; always new and surprising.

Martin Scorsese, 2006. Photo: Fabio Lovino

Katharine Hepburn, 1935. Photo: Ernest Bachrach

Gérard Philipe, 1954. Photo: Everett Collection

Legend tells us that **Robert Mitchum** was never very interested in the screenplays that he was asked to perform. 'Until' – he used to say – 'I got to page 20, there's always someone at that point who gives me a good working over.' With his impressive physique, strong jawline and slightly weary gaze, he seemed a man predestined to play the roles of the defeated, the lost and the naive; in short, roles that seemed carved out to drive his character to destruction. Yet, in his films there was always the sense that he would rise again. And so he did, in a way that very few have been able to do, by staking claim to a certain fragility and a moral integrity, which was a rare currency in Hollywood. His career was not an unblemished success (and he had some brushes with the law), but his unsatisfactory or misconceived films only serve to emphasize the brilliance of his best work: whether as a gangster tormented by his past in *Out of the Past* (1947); the arrogant eroticism he displays in *Macao* (1952); and, from the same year, the melancholic cowboy he plays in *The Lusty Men*; the insane visionary preacher in *The Night of the Hunter* (1955); the course-mannered US Marine in *Heaven Knows, Mr Allison* (1957); the menacing vengeful figure in *Cape Fear* (1962); the drunken sheriff in *El Dorado* (1966); or the detective burdened by a debt of honour in *The Yakuza* (1974). All of these films and many others helped to make Mitchum a true star.

Robert Mitchum, 1946. Photo: Clarence Sinclair Bull

James Cagney, 1935. Photo: John Kobal Foundation

Charles Laughton, 1932. Photo: William Walling Jr.

He was beautiful, elegant and distinguished. **Cary Grant** was also an Englishman, and, above all, he was a great actor, entirely at ease not only in the sophisticated roles that made him famous, but in all types of films. He could never be dull, certainly not in those parts where farce was always in danger of breaking out, or when he was playing an oddball character. Not everyone could keep their dignity as he did in *She Done Him Wrong* (1933), when Mae West said she hadn't been born with handcuffs on, retorting, 'A lot of men would've been safer if you had.' And hearing her reply, 'Oh, I don't know – hands ain't everything.' Or, when Howard Hawks had Grant disguise himself as an American nurse in order to stay with the woman he has just married (*I Was a Male War Bride*, 1949). He was initially compared to Gary Cooper, but with *The Awful Truth* (1937), *Holiday* (1938), *Bringing Up Baby* (1938) and *The Philadelphia Story* (1940), he became the undisputed king of sophisticated comedy, showing himself to be completely at home with its particular rhythms, and to have a talent for blending naivety with irony, innocence with (elegant) perversion. And we should not forget the more serious and dramatic side of his character that, as Alfred Hitchcock understood so well, he could bring to his performances; nor the magnetism or unexpected and highly convincing tension that he could create, especially when his characters confronted danger.

Cary Grant, 1935. Photo: Robert Coburn

'In Hollywood, I was a pretty flibbertigibbet whose charm for the executive department decreased with every increase in her fan-mail. In Berlin, I stepped onto the station platform to meet Pabst and became an actress.... Everywhere I was treated with a kind of decency and respect unknown to me in Hollywood.' So wrote **Louise Brooks** in her memoires.

She was probably the most unconventional actress in the history of cinema, and certainly the most open and unpredictable. She was prepared to leave Paramount Pictures for Germany (to play a troubled and seductive girl in the film *Pandora's Box*, adapted from the play by Franz Wedekind), and then to retire while still relatively young from a world that she no longer felt was her own. Those who had placed her under contract soon forgot her, but those who had admired her on screen certainly did not, entranced by her pure white body, disturbing gaze and ultra-black bobbed hairstyle. She was a dazzling, unforgettable beauty, muse to the surrealists and iconic screen legend.

Louise Brooks, 1928. Photo: Eugene Robert Richee

Elizabeth Taylor, 1948. Photo: Philippe Halsman

Gene Tierney, 1946. Photo: Album

Alfred Hitchcock simply loved to be seen, to an almost narcissistic degree. It may have been his way of counteracting a physical image that was far from elegant. He was not the first director to 'put himself in the picture', but he was certainly the one who did it with the greatest determination and regularity (almost forty times). In the end it became a kind of highly personal movie hallmark. But his willingness to appear in front of the lens was not limited to film, and he often posed to publicize his own work, as in the case of *The Birds* (1963), when he gave his imagination free range. In this photo he was playing on another of his trademarks: his passion for enormous cigars. He also had himself filmed seated at a table, engaged in picking clean the bones of a succulent roast fowl.

It would be superficial, however, to see these as mere instances of vanity. They are, instead, testament to his devotion to his work and to his conception of cinema: 'pieces of cake' was how he often defined his films. This was his way of emphasizing the pleasure and entertainment that cinema should be able to give its audience. It made perfect sense for him to make jokes about his own plump silhouette or to be ironic (as in the case of *The Birds*), especially considering that his films were quite capable, at any moment, of overturning the harmony of the world.

Alfred Hitchcock, 1962. Photo: Philippe Halsman

Lauren Bacall, 1944. Photo: Album

Shirley MacLaine, *c.* 1960. Photo: Album

Okay, so she couldn't act, but she was sensational. That's what they said about **Ava Gardner**. Without doubt she was the most beautiful of them all. Her slightly exotic look, the perfect oval of her face, made her the ultimate manifestation of a goddess on Earth – she could bewitch and seduce with just a hint of a smile or a heavily laden glance.

Gardner owed everything to her physical charms, to her image and to her wonderful relationship with the camera and with photographers. In fact, a portrait taken by her brother-in-law, Larry Tarr, and displayed in the front window of his studio, was all it took to change the destiny of this girl from North Carolina. That photo was seen by talent scouts who tracked her down, and the rest is Hollywood history.

Some of her most unforgettable roles are perhaps more memorable for her thrilling presence than for her acting abilities (*The Snows of Kilimanjaro*, 1952; *Mogambo*, 1953; *The Barefoot Contessa*, 1954; *On the Beach*, 1959), up until her last great appearances made possible for her by John Huston (*The Bible*, 1966; *The Life and Times of Judge Roy Bean*, 1972), when alcohol and a life lived perhaps too intensely had already left their tell-tale marks on her splendid features.

Her legendary beauty was accompanied by a reputation for being a promiscuous man-eater, earned because of her stormy relationships and brief tempestuous marriages: to Mickey Rooney, whom she married in January 1942 only to divorce a year later; to Frank Sinatra, the details of which filled the glossy magazines until the sensation caused by their divorce. It was the same with so many of her other short and fiery affairs, such as her relationship with the Italian actor Walter Chiari, for instance.

The great photographer, Philippe Halsman, was famous for inventing unusual and original solutions for each of his photo sessions, and he chose to portray Ava Gardner in the simplest way possible, virtually unadorned: in close-up with a lock of hair covering part of her face, it is almost as if the actress had turned away from the shot, in a moment of distraction. Her true beauty needed no other framing.

Ava Gardner, 1954. Photo: Philippe Halsman

Antonio Banderas, 2008. Photo: Paola Kudacki

Jeremy Irons, 1990. Photo: Michel Comte

Michael Caine, 1965. Photo: David Hurn

Peter O'Toole, 1962. Photo: David Hurn

Claudia Cardinale in *8 1/2*, directed by Federico Fellini, 1962. Photo: Paul Ronald

Marcello Mastroianni in *8 1/2*, directed by Federico Fellini, 1962. Photo: Paul Ronald

Rebel or misfit? Hero or victim? Twenty-four years of life, three films (*East of Eden*, *Rebel Without a Cause* and *Giant*), a violent death and a thwarted love (for the Italian actress, Anna Maria Pierangeli) have all helped build one of Hollywood's most enduring myths, **James Dean**. His life contributed to an immaculate image: the loss, when he was very young, of his mother; the dramatic conflicts with his father; it is no surprise that we identify Dean with the characters he played. First, he was the fragile and complex Cal Trask, divided between a puritanical father and an absent (and 'immoral') mother; then the angry and dissatisfied Jim Stark, a character who could have had everything in life and, instead, ends up ruining it all. He added little to his myth as the co-star in *Giant*, playing a landowner made rich by the discovery of oil, but ruined by success, but by this time Dean was already an icon in an America filled with false self-confidence. Millions of young men learned to imitate his tics, to emphasize their own fragility, and to dress against all the rules, wearing just jeans, no tie, and a sweater to enhance a kind of scruffy exhibitionism…. After all those grown-up and virile stars, who could resist the new era of defenceless, restless anti-heroes, whose worlds were filled with circling wolves, and who were not ashamed to cry or suffer?

James Dean, 1955. Photo: Phil Stern/CPI

Bette Davis, 1939. Photo: George Hurrell

Greta Garbo, 1932. Photo: George Fitzmaurice

Jean Marais, 1995. Photo: Serge Cohen

Isabelle Huppert, 1994. Photo: Henri Cartier-Bresson

Towards the end of *Roma*, the film-portrait that Fellini dedicated to the Eternal City in 1972, the camera intercepts **Anna Magnani** on her way home to Trastevere on the west bank of the Tiber, and off-screen the director's unmistakable voice describes the actress to the audience: 'Anna Magnani would be perfect as a symbol of Rome, a Rome seen as a she-wolf or a Vestal virgin, an aristocratic beggar woman, both sad and clown-like.' The actress stops the director's eulogy and takes leave of the audience by slamming her front door in their faces, but it is undeniable that these words were sincerely meant. And, above all, true. Even in Hollywood (where she won an Oscar for *The Rose Tattoo*), Magnani did not try to hide her more Italian, more Roman, side: her unique and unforgettable 'normality' that made her so credible in the heart-breaking role of Sister Pina, the working class woman in *Roma città aperta* (Rome Open City); in her touching monologue in *Voce umana* (The Human Voice); in the garb of a rabble-rousing figure in *L'onorevole Angelina* (The Honourable Angelina), as a *commedia dell'arte* actress in *Le Carrosse d'or* (The Golden Coach), or as a woman of the underclass in *Mamma Roma*. She was always the same, always different, always superb.

Anna Magnani, 1951. Photo: Philippe Halsman

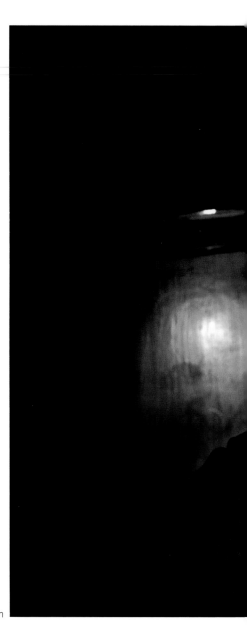

Sean Penn, 2008. Photo: Paolo Pellegrin

Penélope Cruz, 2008. Photo: Raymond Meier

Angelina Jolie, 2004. Photo: Martin Schoeller

Every portrait should conceal a story, whether great or small, it doesn't really matter. It should be the story of a special relationship, of a spark that is about to burst into flame and create a short circuit between the photographer and his subject; between the person with his finger on the shutter and the one being captured.

It is part of the photographer's art to learn not just how to control the lights and master all the technical aspects involved, but also to understand in just a few minutes who the person in front of him really is, what character traits could be drawn out, and quietly to persuade him or her to begin to interact with the camera – a game of invention and complicity.

Fabio Lovino remembers very well, and with a great deal of amusement, **Daniel Auteuil**'s visit to his studio in the heart of Rome. For this French actor, born and raised in the theatres where his opera singer parents worked, stage sets and make-believe are simply part of his everyday life. With great courtesy and curiosity, he began to walk around under the studio's high glass roof. Quite naturally, he followed his instincts and the game began. Lovino photographed him and together they created a rather sinister figure, a tough guy with a confrontational expression on his face, a bare chest and a cigarette stuck between his lips; the tattoo-like sticker stuck on his shoulder bears the slogan 'fumer tue' ('smoking kills').

Daniel Auteuil, 2004. Photo: Fabio Lovino

Ben Kingsley, 2003. Photo: Gino Sprio

Paul Newman, 2000. Photo: Bruce Davidson

LA PLUS BELLE

DU SIÈCLE : Holin,
de F

'Full of fire under the ice' was how Alfred Hitchcock summed her up, and although he may not have been the director who discovered **Grace Kelly**, it was certainly he who made her one of the stars of Hollywood. He was referring to that magical contrast between her icy, almost too-perfect beauty and the sensual charge that gave her such an impact on screen. She certainly made an impact on the imagination of the master of the thriller genre, who, after having used her as the victim of a treacherous husband in *Dial M for Murder*, made her the embodiment of his feminine ideal: blonde, elegant, cool, but also resourceful and naturally provocative. Who does not remember the grace (and hint of mischievousness) with which she draws out a diaphanous nightdress from the tiniest of valises in *Rear Window*? Or how she seduces 'The Cat', played by Cary Grant, in *To Catch a Thief*, against the backdrop of a firework display that emphasizes the explosive sensual side of her nature? Behind those perfect features and beautiful manners (she was the daughter of one of the richest families in Philadelphia) there burned an all-consuming passion, and cinema still remembers her for this in *The Country Girl* (for which she won an Oscar) and *High Society*. But marriage to Prince Rainier of Monaco brought a career that had given such pleasure to an end, and she took up a new role, a royal one.

Previous pages: Jean-Paul Belmondo, 1968. Photo: Raymond Depardon

Grace Kelly, 1954. Photo: Philippe Halsman

Tilda Swinton, 1999. Photo: Fabio Lovino

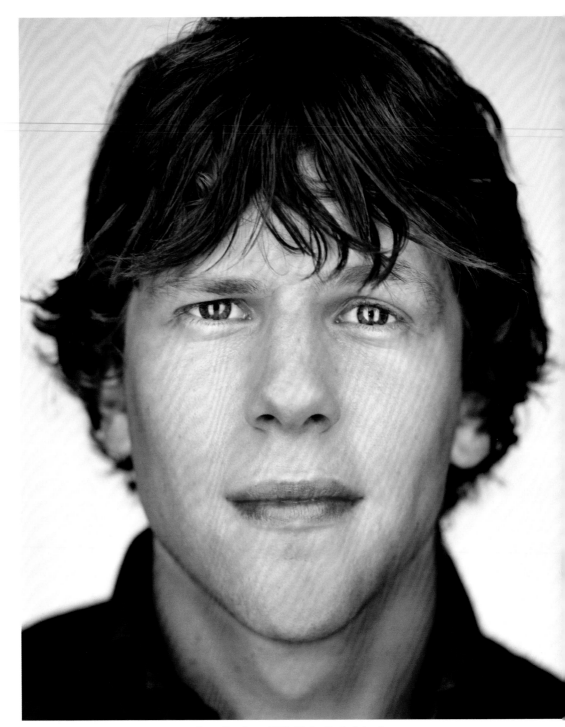

Jesse Eisenberg, 2010. Photo: Martin Schoeller

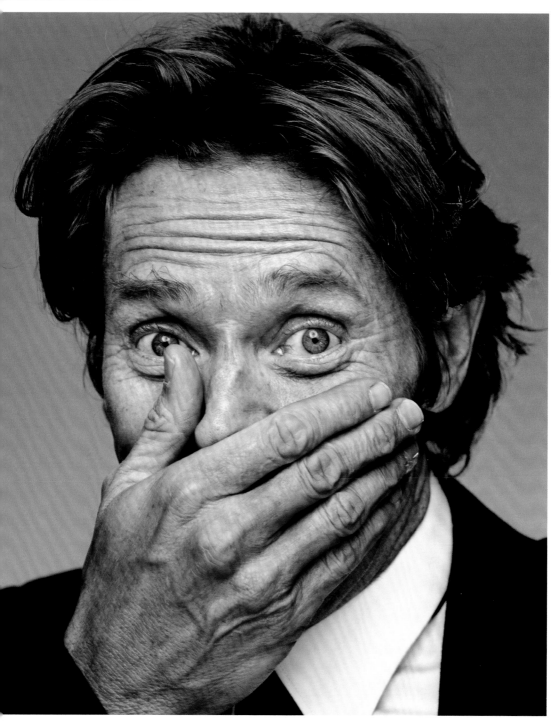

Willem Dafoe, 2009. Photo: Martin Schoeller

What does an actor new to cinema ask himself when called upon to play a man of the new millennium, to get to grips with a whole series of insecurities and neuroses, both personal and social, which threaten every certainty? How can one adapt sufficiently in order to mould one's mind, one's language and sometimes one's own body to give life to these very insecurities and neuroses with psychologically dense and multifaceted performances?

There is a new generation of actors who can take on these elements, who are able to act with a light touch, without overloading the emphasis on a character: and **Christian Bale** is the archetypal representative of this generation.

Few other actors are able to put their own bodies through the number of changes that he has, be it losing or gaining weight, building up powerful muscles or altering his actual physical features in order to enter into a character and make him believable (as can be seen from his performances in films such as *The Machinist*, *Batman Begins*, *Rescue Dawn* and *The Fighter*).

It is true that one needs a certain aptitude and a little good luck (in Bale's case he was helped by the fact that he comes from a family of travelling performers – his mother was a circus artiste, his grandfather was a magician and ventriloquist), but sensitivity is the greatest gift that anyone who wants to play out stories of the complexity of modern life could ask for. It is this sensitivity that allows the actor to carry within himself a whole raft of emotions and authentic feelings. And even if they are not actually lived, at least they appear to be real in cinematic fiction.

Christian Bale, 2000. Photo: Martin Schoeller

LOCATIONS

Actually, the thing most accurately portrayed in the Western is the land. I think you can say that the real star of my Westerns has always been the land.

John Ford

New York; *Once Upon a Time in America*, directed by Sergio Leone, 1984.
Photo: Ladd Company/Album

Berlin; *The Big Lift*, directed by George Seaton, 1950.
Photo: 20th Century Fox

John Ford was quite certain that no studio, no matter how well furnished and full of spotlights, could ever equate with the beauty and light of the wide open spaces. What could be better than the great rocks sculpted by the centuries in Monument Valley as a setting of an Indian attack, or the route of a stagecoach? Or for building a frontier town filled with saloons, or the O.K. Corral? No one in Hollywood would have been able to 'fake' those leaden looming clouds that from time to time cast an unexpected shadow over the figures of his heroes, as happens to Captain Nathan Brittles (played by John Wayne), delivering his monologue over his wife's grave in *She Wore a Yellow Ribbon*. No special effect could ever have achieved such dramatic meteorological perfection. Filming far away from Hollywood and its vast studio buildings was much more satisfactory.

Conversely, there are directors and producers ready to wager that no natural environment could ever equal that which they could 'construct' in the studio. Where in nature could one find a fiery red sunset like the one which lights up the last scene of *Gone with the Wind*? Only the combined genius of the set designer William Cameron Menzies and the cinematographers Ernest Haller and Lee Garmes (aided by the visionary genius of the producer David O. Selznick) could have created what is one of the most famous 'exterior scenes' in the history of cinema.

The curious thing is that the development of technology has not altered the terms of the debate, and if anything it has heightened it, because the possibility of digitally altering every kind of finished image still leaves the director (or the producer) with the same question: where to shoot? Out-of-doors or in the studio? From real life or on a set? Certainly, the times when, in order to create a realistic setting for a scene in the first Indiana Jones film, it was necessary to take down all the television aerials from the roofs of a town, are gone forever. All one needs today is some good software to retouch the image. But this does not take away from the fascination with the richness of nature that in some ways is still inaccessible even to the most advanced technologies. It is impossible to imagine any road movie without budgeting for long scenes shot outdoors. The weather, though, like the heart, will not be ruled, and if the Rain God decides to put a spoke in the wheels

Beijing; *The Last Emperor*, directed by Bernardo Bertolucci, 1987. Photo: Columbia Pictures

Paris; *The Red Balloon*, directed by Albert Lamorisse, 1956. Photo: Everett Collection

of a production, no counter-charm or propitiatory dance will make any difference.

It is because of this that Hollywood's moguls took the decision to reconstruct everything in the studio, encouraging the development of a generation of set designers who revolutionized ways of filming, from Cedric Gibson to Ken Adam and Dante Ferretti. But by building sets, the sense of adventure is often lost, and this is something that at times has spurred even the most famous directors to take up decidedly odd proposals simply because the filming will be done in exotic and unusual places. From this point of view, John Huston was a true pioneer of the cinematic journey and of exploring faraway settings, including Ravello on the Amalfi Coast, where he was based for the writing and filming of *Beat the Devil* together with Truman Capote and Humphrey Bogart. It is not known if he was more inspired by the presence of Gina Lollobrigida (the star of the film) or by the abundant supplies of whiskey (as Capote's version of events tends to suggest).

But one doesn't *have* to travel very far, and sometimes it really is enough just to go round the corner to find a truly unusual setting, one which is both credible and original. We may have seen it countless times, the black bulk of the Brooklyn Bridge set against a white sky, shot by Gordon Willis (cinematographer) and Woody Allen (director), but it is that bench in the foreground which we find unforgettable. Or how about the Champs Elysées, filmed by Raoul Coutard under Jean-Luc Godard's direction as the backdrop to the love affair between Jean-Paul Belmondo and Jean Seberg. And even when the Trevi Fountain received Anita Ekberg in *La dolce vita* it took on an original, almost magical power, so very different from the souvenir images treasured by tourists from all over the world. In the end, the real issue is not what is being filmed, but how it is being filmed….

P.M.

Chevy Chase in Monument Valley; *National Lampoon's Vacation*, directed by Harold Ramis, 1983. Photo: Warner Brothers

Previous pages: Monument Valley; *Stagecoach*, directed by John Ford, 1939. Photo: Everett Collection

Monument Valley; *Winged Migration*, directed by Jacques Perrin, 2001. Photo: Everett Collection

Robert De Niro in Las Vegas; *Casino*, directed by Martin Scorsese, 1995. Photo: Universal

Sharon Stone in Las Vegas; *Casino*, directed by Martin Scorsese, 1995. Photo: Universal

Las Vegas; *One from the Heart*, directed by Francis Ford Coppola, 1982. Photo: Columbia Pictures

Robert Redford in Las Vegas; *The Electric Horseman*, directed by Sydney Pollack, 1979. Photo: Everett Collection

Overleaf: Anna Magnani in Rome; *Mamma Roma*, directed by Pier Paolo Pasolini, 1962. Photo: A. Palma Archive

Audrey Hepburn and Gregory Peck in Rome; *Roman Holiday*, directed by William Wyler, 1953. Photo: GBB Archive

Marcello Mastroianni and Anita Ekberg in Rome; *La dolce vita*, directed by Federico Fellini, 1960. Photo: Pierluigi Praturlon

Katharine Hepburn and Rossano Brazzi in
Venice; *Summertime*, directed by David Lean,
1955. Photo: Everett Collection

Venice; *Casanova*, directed by Lasse Hallström, 2005. Photo: Touchstone

Venice; *Death in Venice*, directed by Luchino Visconti, 1971. Photo: Everett Collection

New York; *The Day After Tomorrow*, directed by Roland Emmerich, 2004. Photo: 20th Century Fox

Woody Allen and Diane Keaton in New York;
Manhattan, directed by Woody Allen, 1979.
Photo: Everett Collection

Which is better? The **Paris** recreated in the studio by Marcel Carné and Jacques Prévert for *Hôtel du Nord* and *Le jour se lève*, where the sets designed by Alexandre Trauner gave form to the spaces and streets that come to reflect human feelings, or the version of the real city shot by the Nouvelle Vague, where the geography of the city becomes a part of cinema due to the concrete nature of its streets, corners and facades? One can argue either way, be it as a setting for human emotions (as Truffaut uses it), or as a theatre in which human destinies are played out (as in the films of Claude Autant-Lara or Julien Duvivier), or as the backdrop to a documentary examination (as it is for Agnès Varda) or an offstage scene that conceals mysterious shadows (as in the noir films of Jean-Pierre Melville).

It seems that cinema only needs a little freedom and even the most picture-postcard image of the Champs Elysées can inspire the most unconventional of directors, as in *À bout de souffle* (Breathless) by Jean-Luc Godard. Or perhaps the version of Paris reinvented by Hollywood is better still, as directors as varied as Ernst Lubitsch and Stanley Donen, Billy Wilder and Vincent Minnelli, and even Roman Polanski and Woody Allen have all sought out the myth of the city by giving it a new face and a new geography each time.

Jean-Paul Belmondo and Jean Seberg in Paris; *À bout de souffle* (Breathless), directed by Jean-Luc Godard, 1960.
Photo: Everett Collection

voix et guitares du monde
Carole Fredericks
John McLaughlin
Dianne Reeves
Lucky Peterson
04 75 01 27 30
ALLAN - ANCONE - CHATEAUNEUF DU RHONE - LA COUCOURDE - SAUZET - SAVASSE

Audrey Tautou in Paris; *Amélie*, directed by Jean-Pierre Jeunet, 2001. Photo: Everett Collection

Carey Mulligan and Peter Sarsgaard in Paris; *An Education*, directed by Lone Scherfig, 2009. Photo: Kerry Brown

Van Johnson and Elizabeth Taylor in Paris; *The Last Time I Saw Paris*, directed by Richard Brooks, 1954.

Photo: Everett Collection

In cinema, no other city owes so much to its own history as **Berlin**. Because no other city has been interrogated and dissected so minutely by its directors. It is no easy matter to set a film in Berlin: account has to be taken of its image, of its rulers, of its winners and losers. In its long and linear history, Berlin has seen revolutions, civil disturbances and violent shocks where each one seems to demand that all traces of the previous regime should be wiped out. Perhaps it was not so much the city itself, but the idea of the city and its images, that inspired the film *Berlin: Die Sinfonie der Grosstadt* (Berlin: Symphony of a Metropolis) (1927), which was much more of a film-essay than a documentary. And this is what has made the city a palimpsest of our collective memories, as they are reflected in each successive image which is then always cut off from its own roots: the Weimar Republic, the Nazi period, the Second World War, the hardship of reconstruction, the East/West division, the collapse of the Wall. Only the angels, perhaps, could hope to be able to weave together all its stories in a single vision. But to do so would mean taking to the skies over Berlin on *Wings of Desire*....

Ulrich Mühe in Berlin; *The Lives of Others*, directed by Florian Henckel von Donnersmarck, 2006.
Photo: Sony Pictures Classics

Michael Caine in Berlin; *Funeral in Berlin*, directed by Guy Hamilton, 1966. Photo: Everett Collection

Bruno Ganz in Berlin; *Wings of Desire*, directed by Wim Wenders, 1987. Photo: Everett Collection

Tokyo; *Babel*, directed by Alejandro González Iñárritu, 2006. Photo: Paramount Pictures

Miho Nikaido in Tokyo; *Tokyo Decadence*, directed by Ryu Murakami, 1992. Photo: Everett Collection

Lucas Black in Tokyo; *The Fast and the Furious: Tokyo Drift*, directed by Justin Lin, 2006. Photo: Universal

Using a gentle watercolour palette and the combined popularity of Donald Duck, José Carioca the Brazilian parrot and Panchito Pistoles the Mexican rooster, Walt Disney reinvented Latin America for propaganda purposes. It was in the mid-1940s, and it was essential to divert this region away from Nazi influence. This was a special request from Nelson Rockefeller and, where even Orson Welles and his film *It's All True* had failed, it took cartoons to succeed in securing the sympathy of the South American 'cousins', who were not always well disposed towards the Yankees. Donald Duck had already had an outing in 1942 with *Saludos Amigos*. In 1945 another attempt was made to neutralize any potential hostility with *The Three Caballeros*, which included his dancing the samba with Brazilian entertainer Aurora Miranda, courting (very politely) the beautiful bathers of Acapulco, and the scene when he turns into a sweet-toothed bee pursuing dancer Carmen Molina while singing *You Belong to My Heart* from the centre of a flower. These films are miracles of beauty and invention, such as only Walt Disney could create, where reality is transformed into an explosion of sound and colour, and before our very eyes drawings magically come to life.

In this animated film the city of **Rio de Janeiro** is signified by the black and white waves on the pavements of the Copacabana promenade. And even just a walk along the most famous beach in the world to a samba rhythm, effortlessly constructs the exotic myth, redolent of tropical beauty, of a city like Rio.

Rio de Janeiro; *Saludos Amigos*, directed by Walt Disney, 1942. Photo: Everett Collection

THE
BUILD-UP

Pick up a camera. Shoot something. No matter how small, no matter how cheesy, no matter whether your friends and your sister star in it. Put your name on it as director. Now you're a director. Everything after that you're just negotiating your budget and your fee.

James Cameron

Ridley Scott on the set of *Blade Runner*, 1962. Photo: Sunset Boulevard

Production designer Cedric Gibbons (left) works on his designs, 1942. Photo: Walter Sanders

Director Anthony Mann oversees the models for a scene from *The Fall of the Roman Empire*, 1964.
Photo: Everett Collection

Overleaf: The Sicilian town of Bagheria was recreated in Ben Arous, Tunisia, by production designer Maurizio Sabatini for the film *Baarìa*, directed by Giuseppe Tornatore, 2008. Photo: Emanuele Scorcelletti

The ancient Rome set at Cinecittà Studios in Rome, 2009. Photo: Massimo Siragusa

A storage area for statues at Cinecittà Studios in Rome, 2009. Photo: Massimo Siragusa

Costume designer Walter Plunkett with Vivien Leigh on the set of *Gone with the Wind*, directed by Victor Fleming, 1939.
Photo: John Kobal Foundation

Costume designer Milo Anderson shows Olivia de Havilland the costume designs for *Captain Blood*,
directed by Michael Curtiz, 1935. Photo: Everett Collection

Divas they may be, but at heart they are all human, and therefore, imperfect. Ultimately destined to be adored, they must wait for a great costumier to emphasize their gifts and hide any defects.

And **Adrian** had no equal. Hollywood history tells that his first great success came when he designed a dress with a triangular outline for Joan Crawford, who was endowed with particularly broad shoulders and slightly short legs, for the film *Letty Lynton* (1932). It camouflaged her somewhat masculine physique while highlighting all of her alluring feminine perfection. 'Who would ever have believed that my career rested entirely on Crawford's shoulders?' Adrian used to joke; but she wasn't his only client.

Greta Garbo's hats (including the extraordinary French-style hat, so out of character for a Soviet functionary, that she wore in *Ninotchka* (1939)) were designed by Adrian and turned the ice-cool Swedish diva into a true icon of glamour. Adrian was also responsible for the famous red shoes worn by Judy Garland in *The Wizard of Oz* (1939).

For each film, the costume designer has to imagine a style, and construct a personality. Cecil Beaton, that famous photographer and talented costume designer, was inspired by the languid photographs taken by the young Jacques Henri Lartigue in Belle Époque Paris for his designs for *My Fair Lady* (1964). Walter Plunkett, another prolific costume designer, created a whole series of costumes for *Gone with the Wind* (1939) that accompanied Scarlett O'Hara throughout her evolution from vivacious Southern belle to a woman hardened by war and by life itself, and who said the famous line, 'Tomorrow is another day', in the final scene of the film.

Every costume designer is tempted to escape from the world of film sets, with all their pressures of time and plotlines that must be respected, and become a designer who is in charge of all the effects. Adrian was able to realize his dream in the 1940s and had great success when he opened his own fashion atelier where the self-same divas, whom he had dressed for the make-believe of the cinema, now came to ask him to provide them with clothes for their off-screen lives. And so they could, more than ever, be dressed to impress in both public and private.

Overleaf: Sharon Stone at a costume fitting, 2006. Photo: Art Streiber

Costume designer Adrian, *c.* 1930. Photo: John Kobal Foundation

'Animation can explain whatever the mind of man can conceive. This facility makes it the most versatile and explicit means of communication yet devised for quick mass appreciation.'

The young Walter Disney, born in Chicago in 1901, always wanted to work in cinema. He even dreamt of collaborating with Charlie Chaplin, but a chance meeting with a talented animator led him to change direction and produce his first advertising cartoon strips – which already contained the embryonic form of what would become the core of his later films. With time, experimentation and the frequent invention of new techniques, his stories and characters came to life, from Oswald the Lucky Rabbit (1927) to his distant cousin, virtually identical except that his ears were rounded instead of pointed, Mortimer Mouse, subsequently rechristened Mickey Mouse. The latter appeared on screens in 1928 in the first animated short film with a sound accompaniment, *Steamboat Willie*.

To become **Walt Disney** takes technical expertise, as well as talent, but a strong visionary ability is also essential. You first need to have a dream and then you need to have the means of realizing it. In the early 1930s Disney decided to create a full-length animated film, complete with a sound track and new techniques. It was more than a dream, it seemed like madness, and it was all the more costly for that, nearly bankrupting the studio. Disney later complained, 'I'd say it's been my biggest problem all my life…it's money. It takes a lot of money to make these dreams come true.'

But at last, in December 1937 in a cinema in Los Angeles, *Snow White and the Seven Dwarfs* was screened for the first time: it was an enormous success and the audience gave it a standing ovation. And so an empire and a cinematographic language were born: the world of Walt Disney.

Walt Disney examines the storyboards for *Alice in Wonderland* with director Wilfred Jackson, 1951.
Photo: Everett Collection

Erich Von Stroheim, *c.* 1944. Photo: John Kobal Foundation

Joseph Losey, 1965. Photo: Eve Arnold

Nimble, elegant and impeccably dressed, he could dance with grace on screen without the need for grand sets. With clever choreography, which he often devised himself, he could create an effect, for example, with a hat stand and a group of lookalikes ready to 'fall down' one after another, as in his famous dance routine in *Top Hat* (1935). Accompanied by just his shadow, or even without it, he could carry on his exhilarating tap dancing up a wall and across a ceiling in defiance of every law of gravity.

George Balanchine and Rudolph Nureyev considered **Fred Astaire** to be the greatest dancer of the twentieth century; certainly he was the most gifted dancer in musical comedies, and although he lacked the muscular strength and tone that distinguished Gene Kelly, he still had great flexibility and a sensitive, polished charm.

The son of an Austrian Jew who converted to Catholicism and an American descendant of German Lutheran immigrants, Frederick Austerlitz (Astaire's real name) brought to dance, and to cinema, a certain flavour of vaudeville which is very much part of a Middle European tradition. And if the storylines of the films in which he appeared are only flimsy excuses for his performances, it's his set-pieces, danced either on his own or with his partners – especially the blonde-haired Ginger Rogers – that we still remember.

And behind every pas de deux danced with perfect synchronicity, in splendid costumes, with feathers and swirling skirts and impeccable evening dress, there lay meticulous, obsessive, nerve-shredding preparation. A punishing schedule pushed every aspect of the scenography, choreography and lighting to the very limits of their possibilities. Astaire's perfectionism was legendary and the weeks of intense preparation that preceded filming could become a veritable nightmare for his partners and collaborators. He was never satisfied with his performance, and was always ready to attempt new heights of virtuosity; he claimed that he never felt that he had truly lived up to his full potential. Although, as he confessed, when he saw his films again he didn't think he was too bad.

Overleaf: Dance rehearsals for *West Side Story*, directed by Robert Wise and Jerome Robbins, 1961.
Photo: Phil Stern/CPI

Fred Astaire, *c.* 1945. Photo: John Kobal Foundation

James Dean at a dance lesson given by Katherine Dunham, 1955. Photo: Dennis Stock

Paul Newman at the Actor's Studio in New York, 1955. Photo: Eve Arnold

Marilyn Monroe, 1952.
Photo: Philippe Halsman

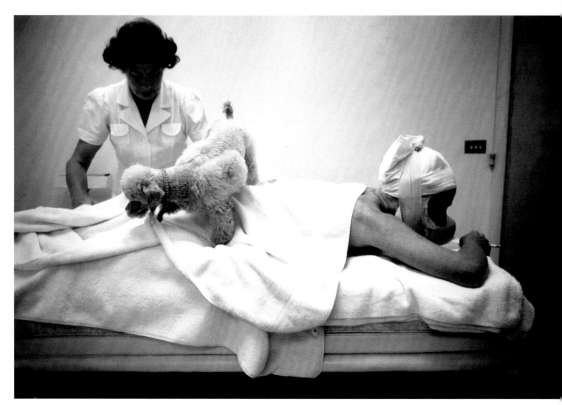

Joan Crawford, 1959. Photo: Eve Arnold

Vidal Sassoon cuts Mia Farrow's hair for *Rosemary's Baby*, directed by Roman Polanski, 1967.
Photo: Bettmann

144

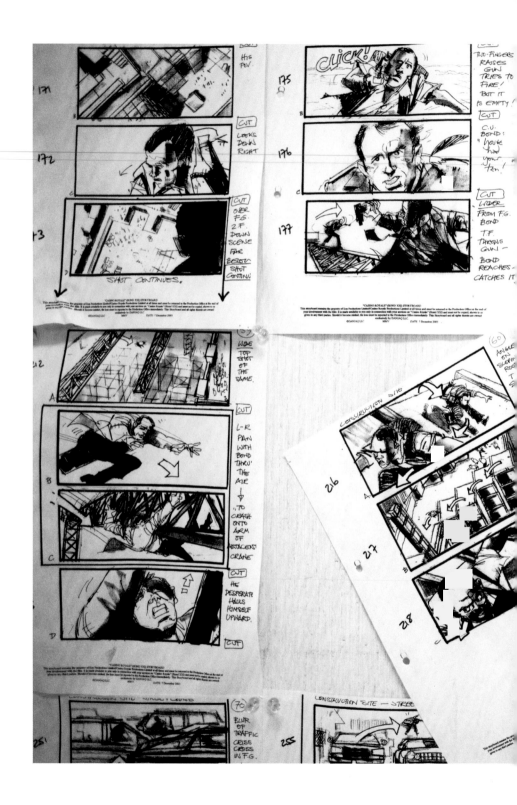

145

Storyboards for the Bond film *Casino Royale*, directed by Martin Campbell, 2006. Photo: Greg Williams

He is engrossed in reading the script during a pause in shooting, and is applying his full concentration as he attempts to engage his memory and get those damned lines into his head, because he will have to recall them later on set.

In this photograph by Eve Arnold, **Clark Gable** has nothing about him of the swashbuckling, slightly blustering hero on which he had built his image. There is nothing left of the journalist hunting down a scoop from *It Happened One Night* (from 1934 and for which he won an Oscar for his performance); nor is there anything left of the fearless leader of the ship's mutinous crew in *Mutiny on the Bounty* (1935). And, above all, there is nothing of the adventurer and heartbreaker who has risen from nothing, and who understands so well, and apparently better than anyone else, what might be the key to Scarlett O'Hara's heart (it is only she who takes the whole four hours of *Gone with the Wind* (1939) to realize).

Gable's fellow actors appreciated him for his kindly ways and warm personality, even away from the set. Women spoke of it in his marriages, his many affairs, and his great love for the charming Carole Lombard, who left him a widower at the age of 41. The public loved him for being a rough mannered but good-hearted man, who in essence was still not so very different from the young man who had taken a few knocks as he worked his way up the ranks.

But in the last few years of his life his personality changed, his voice softened and his light-toned arrogance made room for a heavier greyness. He had been twice decorated for valour during the Second World War, but now, in the post-war era, he was displaying a certain dismay. On the set of *The Misfits* (1960), where this photograph was taken, Gable was carrying the emotional baggage of his real-life experiences, the wrinkles of a bitter but full maturity accumulated one after another.

It was to be his last performance as he died of a heart attack shortly after the end of filming.

Clark Gable, 1960. Photo: Eve Arnold

Ingmar Bergman, cinematographer Sven Nykvist, Erland Josephsson and Liv Ullman at the director's home in Gotland during the making of *Scenes from a Marriage*, 1972. Photo: Gunnar Lantz

François Truffaut and Jean-Pierre Léaud with the script for *Two English Girls*, 1971.
Photo: Raymond Depardon

Robert Aldrich during the making of *The Flight of the Phoenix*, 1965. Photo: Eve Arnold

Warren Beatty, director Elia Kazan and other actors from *Splendor in the Grass* working on the script, 1961.
Photo: John Kobal Foundation

The first cooperative of cinema artists was born in 1919, founded by the actors Mary Pickford, Douglas Fairbanks, the director D.W. Griffith and by Charlie Chaplin.

The idea was to control the rights, and thus the destinies of those who had thought, written, acted and directed. With **United Artists**, the control remained in the hands of the artists themselves, from the writing of the scripts to the famous 'final cut' that effectively allowed them to have the last word, the final definitive verdict, on the version of the film to be tested on the public. And if the possibility of making money from the films remained in the artists' hands, so too the possibility of making a loss had to be taken into account, an inevitable counterpart to such longed-for independence.

Sharing risks and benefits is never easy to get right, and the early years at United Artists were marked by various problems and corporate readjustments. For example, in order to keep running the company had to produce a certain number of films each year that, in turn, due to a question of equal distribution of costs and profits between the members, had to cost more or less the same amount. But this did not always happen, and while Chaplin decided to take more time producing just a few films each year, Douglas Fairbanks would throw himself into making lavish and vastly expensive costume dramas.

With all its highs and lows, the history of United Artists became an integral part of the history of Hollywood. Nearly thirty years later, a group of photographers led by Robert Capa were to do the same thing for photography. Magnum Photos was founded with an identical vision: to be able to control, forever and in the same way, the images that they produced, the fruit of their own creative work.

Charlie Chaplin, Darryl Zanuck, Sam Goldwin and, seated, Mary Pickford, Joseph M. Schenck and Douglas Fairbanks, 1934.
Photo: Everett Collection

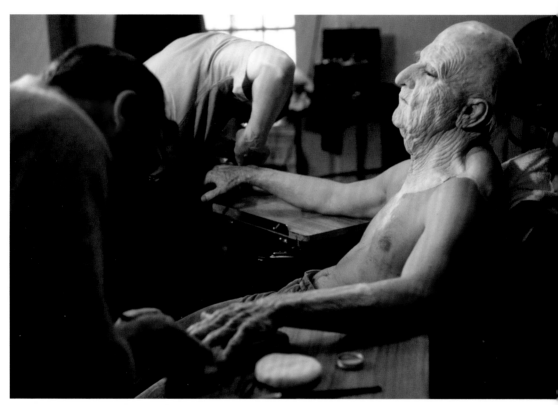

Make-up tests for Dustin Hoffman's character in *Little Big Man*, directed by Arthur Penn, 1969. Photo: Ernst Haas

Sean Connery and Michael Caine check the script of *The Man Who Would Be King*, directed by John Huston, 1975.
Photo: Eve Arnold

A technician moves a scale model of the
Titanic for the film *Raise the Titanic*,
directed by Jerry Jameson, 1980.
Photo: Associated Film Distribution

Terence Stamp and Monica Vitti recording additional dialogue for *Modesty Blaise*, directed by Joseph Losey, 1965.
Photo: Eve Arnold

Overleaf: In the Arizona desert, technicians set the stage for the filming of *The Flight of the Phoenix*,
directed by Robert Aldrich, 1965. Photo: Eve Arnold

Frank Capra in the editing room, 1946. Photo: Rex Hardy

POINT

REA OF ANCIENT LAKE BEDS
TEN MILLION YEARS AGO.
BEEN TILTED AND PUSHED
FORCES, AND ERODED BY WIND
ONTAIN BORATES AND GYPSUM.
INNACLE IS MANLY BEACON.

Michelangelo Antonioni
location hunting for
Zabriskie Point, 1968.
Photo: Bruce Davidson

ACTION!

A director must be a policeman, a midwife,
a psychoanalyst, a sycophant and a bastard.

Billy Wilder

Cecil B. DeMille, 1928. Photo: Everett Collection

James Cameron with Leonardo DiCaprio and Kate Winslet, *Titanic*, 1996. Photo: Album

One could easily feel a little nostalgic for those long gone days when the director, snatching up his megaphone and barking out orders at the extras, could always made a big impression, especially when giving directions to the crew, as Fritz Lang did on the set for *Metropolis* (see overleaf). Megaphones have shrunk today (when they are still used at all) and the director has hoards of assistants and helpers ready to carry out his every wish: so where some of the choreography and even some of the glamour may have been lost, there has certainly been a gain in efficiency. Or so it seems, at least. There is no doubt that on a film set the moment when everything goes quiet and the echo of the clapperboard fades gently into the silence that proceeds the take is the most special and the most magical in the whole process of film-making. It is something that has taken days, sometimes many weeks, to prepare: set-building, costume-making, followed by all the movement, dialogue and light tests. Then, at the director's command, the set and its occupants are transformed into something living, electric, engrossing – into a scene that the viewer will never be able to forget.

It is true that sometimes things do not go smoothly. There are always the stars' tempers, technical problems and the director's doubts, fears, anxieties and excitements. An unplanned shadow, a sudden noise, or an unexpected stammer. Then one hears 'We'll do another take', and everything has to be as it was in the first moment, just like athletes returning to the starting blocks, a little less tense perhaps but certainly just as powerful

and energetic. And as there are no rules, every set is a different story, an unrepeatable adventure, and sometimes one that everyone might want to forget in a hurry. Stanley Kubrick was notorious for pushing his actors to the very limits of exasperation, and was known to reshoot a scene or repeat a line dozens of times. One only needs to ask Tom Cruise and Nicole Kidman, who saw their marriage coming to an end on the set of *Eyes Wide Shut*. And this would seem to be relevant as – it was said – it was actually the director's maniacal perfectionism that pushed the two of them to breaking point.

Clint Eastwood works in a completely different way. When he is shooting it is his intention that virtually the first take should be the right one. He looks for concentration in his actors, a total identification with the character, and he knows very well that this harmony cannot be made to order, or with each snap of the clapperboard. He prefers to rehearse a few times with the actors, but without the camera, and when he sees that they are at ease with their parts, only then does the camera start rolling. His objective is a 'spontaneity' that is certainly constructed, but is not as planned as one might imagine.

Robert Pattinson and Kristen Stewart, *Twilight*, 2008. Photo: David Strick

Alfred Hitchcock with Ingrid Bergman, *Notorious*, 1945. Photo: Robert Capa

These two opposing methods may well be related to the fact that the first director, Stanley Kubrick, had never been an actor; Eastwood, of course, had had a long and distinguished career in that profession. Actor-directors (who are so much closer to the fragility of actors) are generally much more sensitive, less 'dictatorial', and their methods influence their relationship with the whole crew, but not the final result. It is possible to direct great performances with gentleness and with abuse, by shouting or whispering, by pleading or threatening. Vittorio De Sica, who was probably the greatest 'actor–director' in Italian cinema (and we should be grateful to him for transforming Sophia Loren from simply being a curvaceous beauty into an authentic Oscar-winning film star), was famous for playing all the different roles on set, showing everyone, from the lead actor to lowest extra, what they should do. He fused his didactic abilities with a maieutic approach, drawing out his actors' innate abilities. But when, on the set of *The Bicycle Thieves*, he found it was impossible to persuade the young Enzo Staiola to cry on command (and show his distress at his father's misfortunes as he is about to be arrested), De Sica resorted to slipping some cigarette butts into the child's jacket pocket and then accusing him in front of everyone else of being a thief. It achieved the desired effect immediately or, at least, that is the legend.

In the end everything must work perfectly: children cry or laugh, adults perform, the crowd moves, the lights work and the scene is in the can.

P.M.

Cinematographer George Schneiderman, camera operator Burnett Guffey and director John Ford
on the set of *The Iron Horse*, 1924. Photo: Everett Collection

Previous pages: Fritz Lang with a megaphone, directing a scene from *Metropolis*, 1927. Photo: Everett Collection

Sergei Eisenstein at Paramount Studios, 1931. Photo: Eugene Robert Richee

Steven Spielberg, *Jurassic Park*, 1997. Photo: Everett Collection

Previous pages: Cinematographer Charles G. Clarke on the set of *Tarzan and His Mate*, directed by Cedric Gibbons, 1934.
Photo: Everett Collection

Sean Penn directs Emile Hirsch, *Into the Wild*, 2007. Photo: Paramount

Orson Welles in Spain, directing *Falstaff*, 1965. Photo: Nicolas Tikhomiroff

A film must convince, move, tell a story and even be able to prick our consciences. A simple principle perhaps, but in **D.W. Griffith**'s era it was entirely mould-breaking. He was born in Kentucky, David Llewelyn Wark Griffith, the son of a general of the Southern Army in the American Civil War. And perhaps it was the stories of heroic wartime gestures, the deep morals that had guided a nation and inspired its people, which were the life blood that nourished him and that he later tried to convey in his films.

Between 1908 and 1913 Griffith directed about 450 short films (all formatted to the same standard). European cinema was developing at the same time and conceived a different way of exploiting cinematographic fiction.

From his first feature-length film he began to devise a different concept of space and time. In contrast to the usual practice, he did not construct his story through 'pictures', but made anachronistic temporal leaps, although in his films the action progresses coherently in terms of place and time, which, if it seems obvious to us now, represented a real revolution for the time.

The different scenes, the movements of the camera, the use of close-up, the possibility of changing the camera angles, and parallel editing are all elements that Griffith introduced into cinematic practice, and they had all begun as experiments and in response to specific narrative necessities.

The rhythm of his cinematic narrative could be varied. Sometimes it appears rather diffuse, while at other times it is broken up into an exciting string of events. His *Birth of a Nation* (1915), and above all *Intolerance* (1916), are the result of a new way of approaching cinema: with true narrative frescoes, epic undertakings that cost vast sums to produce, grandiose sets and powerful storytelling, all animated by a unique creative impulse. With Griffith's oeuvre, a new figure in cinema was born, one to which we are now quite accustomed, but which he was the first to identify and embody: the figure of the *auteur* director.

D.W. Griffith on the set of one of his films, *c.* 1910. Photo: Bettmann

Nicholas Ray, *55 Days at Peking*, 1962. Photo: Dennis Stock

George Cukor and Greta Garbo, *Two-Faced Woman*, 1941. Photo: Album

'Nobody should try to play comedy unless they have a circus going on inside.'

He had a magic touch, the 'Lubitsch Touch', which meant he could transform each film script into a resounding success, each joke into a pearl of exceptional, intelligent humour. **Ernst Lubitsch** was indisputably the father of American sophisticated comedy.

Born in Berlin in 1892 into a Russian Jewish family, he began his career as an actor around the age of twenty and exhibited a great talent for adapting himself to the most varied roles possible. Cinema soon arrived on the scene, and his precocious technical skills also convinced him, in a very short time, to take his place behind the movie camera and set his signature on all sorts of different films (comedies, costume dramas, Shakespearean tragedies and so on).

In 1920s Hollywood he found his perfect stylistic niche in the talkies, which offered him the possibility of exploiting to the full his innate taste for sly jokiness, for real-life and fictional situations pushed to the limit of paradox, which ensured the success of his most famous films. The updated and invigorated traditions of European theatre, Viennese light opera and vaudeville, found a perfect new home in cinema. And so, thanks to Lubitsch we have learnt to appreciate and recognize the rhythms of comedy, with its semi-musical cadences of dialogue and silence that are still so fresh and pleasing with each reviewing of comedies like *The Shop Around the Corner*; or his greatest creation of all, *The Merry Widow*, a film that has become both a milestone and an example to be imitated by all sophisticated comedies destined for the big screen.

Another European, Billy Wilder, was also a master of comic timing, and admitted to having borrowed freely from the great Ernst Lubitsch. But although Wilder knew how to create films like perfectly oiled machines made up of jokes, characters, entrances and exits, the only person who could say that he had had the honour of seeing his name become an adjective was Lubitsch. And it was an adjective of no small importance, as the critic of the *Chicago Tribune*, Richard Christiansen, wrote some years ago: 'The *Lubitsch Touch* is a brief description that embraces a long list of virtues: sophistication, style, subtlety, wit, charm, elegance, suavity, polished nonchalance and audacious sexual nuance.'

Overleaf: *The Greatest Story Ever Told*, directed by George Stevens, 1963. Photo: Ernst Haas

Ernst Lubitsch, *The Merry Widow*, 1934. Photo: Milton Brown

Pedro Almodóvar, Penélope Cruz and José Luis Gòmez, *Broken Embraces*, 2009. Photo: Album

Meryl Streep with costume designer Patricia Field on the set of *The Devil Wears Prada*, directed by David Frankel, 2006.
Photo: 20th Century Fox

Overleaf: Alfred Hitchcock directing James Stewart and Farley Granger in *Rope*, 1948. Photo: Album

America America, directed by Elia Kazan,
1962. Photo: Constantine Manos

David Lean, *Lawrence of Arabia*, 1962. Photo: Everett Collection

James Stewart on the set of *The Flight of the Phoenix*, directed by Robert Aldrich, 1966. Photo: Phil Stern/CPI

Overleaf: Cinematographer John Alcott adjusts the position of the camera while Stanley Kubrick frames the shot; *2001: A Space Odyssey*, 1966. Photo: Keith Hamshere

Robert Altman, *McCabe and Mrs Miller*, 1971. Photo: Everett Collection

Billy Wilder directs Tony Curtis and Marilyn Monroe in *Some Like It Hot*, 1959. Photo: Everett Collection

The deep relationship between cinema and photography has had some particularly powerful and intense moments. One was when Magnum Photos obtained the exclusive rights to record the different phases of the production of **John Huston**'s film *The Misfits* (1960).

This film was exceptional in every way due to the calibre of the personalities involved. John Huston as director, Arthur Miller as scriptwriter and Marilyn Monroe, Montgomery Clift and Clark Gable as the principal actors, and they were all surrounded by the intense and dazzling light and the endless horizon of the desert around Reno, Nevada, where the director was determined to film nearly all the exterior scenes, as was the practice for Westerns made in the grand manner.

Nine superb photographers took turns behind the stills camera during the filming: Eve Arnold, Cornell Capa, Henri Cartier-Bresson, Bruce Davidson, Elliott Erwitt, Erich Hartmann, Ernst Haas, Inge Morath and Dennis Stock. They were witnesses to the adventure of a film as it was being made, an adventure which they captured day by day, but also to a crucial episode in cinema history that saw the interweaving of private destinies and public personalities while cinema itself was rapidly and ineluctably changing.

The story of this group of misfits (as indicated by the film's title) who find themselves in a desert outpost, in an almost timeless place, seems like a contemporary rereading, both despairing and anachronistic, of the American conquest of the West. And the overlapping between the private affairs of the characters and the actors portraying them has a rather bitter taste when one considers that *The Misfits* was to be the last performance for Marilyn Monroe (she died two years later, in 1962) and for Clark Gable (he was struck down by a heart attack only 15 days after the end of filming).

It is perhaps not a perfect film, but *The Misfits* signals the end of one era and the beginning of a new kind of modernity in cinema: a modernity in which the myths of the past can no longer survive.

Overleaf: Akira Kurosawa, *Ran*, 1984. Photo: Gérard Rancinan

The cast and crew of *The Misfits*, directed by John Huston. From the back: Arthur Miller, producer Frank E. Taylor, Eli Wallach, John Huston, Montgomery Clift, Marilyn Monroe and Clark Gable, 1960. Photo: Elliott Erwitt

'*1900* is an extremely regional film, soaked in popular culture, and yet all in all it is also very much a Hollywood film.'

Bernardo Bertolucci talks of his most personal film, one which is soaked in familial and ancestral memories, as an extremely special work, permeated by a deeply provincial atmosphere where one may not be able to hear the 'bells of history', but where instead everything seems to flow along without ever changing. And yet, in this rarefied atmosphere, Bertolucci has managed to produce a universal film that, precisely because it is authentic and visceral, can be understood by all people in all places. The sprawling tale of the young Olmo, a peasant born in the Emilian countryside on 27 January 1901, which as luck would have it means that he has the same birthday as his landlord, Alfredo, is told with the breadth of an epic, and the half century that the film encapsulates, including peasant revolts, world wars, totalitarianism and the struggle for freedom, becomes the story of our Western world and the romance of the moulding of European man.

The experience of filming *1900* resembled that of other films that try, as honestly as possible, to resemble real life in every way. When this is achieved, with all necessary simplicity, then masterpieces are created. As Bertolucci later recalled, 'When I was filming *1900* everything changed slowly: the countryside, the seasons, the actors, the crew, my face. Life flowed on and film continued on as if it would never end. After a year of shooting, living and filming had become the same thing and I, without realizing it, no longer wanted the film to end.'

Bernardo Bertolucci and Robert De Niro on the set of *1900*, 1974. Photo: Mauro Galligani

Roberto Rossellini, *The Flowers of St Francis*, 1950. Photo: David Seymour

Luchino Visconti, *Rocco and His Brothers*, 1960. Photo: TCI Archive

Alberto Sordi on the set of *Mafioso*, directed by Alberto Lattuada, 1962. Photo: Ferdinando Scianna

Overleaf: Federico Fellini and Marcello Mastroianni, *8 1/2*, 1962. Photo: Tazio Secchiaroli

Vittorio De Sica, *The Last Judgment*, 1959. Photo: Herbert List

Cinematographer Raoul Coutard (left) with Jean-Luc Godard (centre), 1966. Photo: Bruno Barbey

Oscar Werner and François Truffaut, *Fahrenheit 451*, 1966. Photo: Philippe Halsman

Rainer Werner Fassbinder and Hanna Schygulla, 1980. Photo: Everett Collection

Previous pages: Glauber Rocha (right), *Entranced Earth*, Rio de Janeiro, 1966. Photo: René Burri

Cate Blanchett as *Elizabeth*, directed by Shekhar Kapur, 1998. Photo: Greg Williams

Overleaf: Lunch break at Cinecittà Studios, 1996. Photo: Angelo Turetta

Ken Russell directs Vanessa Redgrave in *The Devils*, 1970. Photo: David Hurn

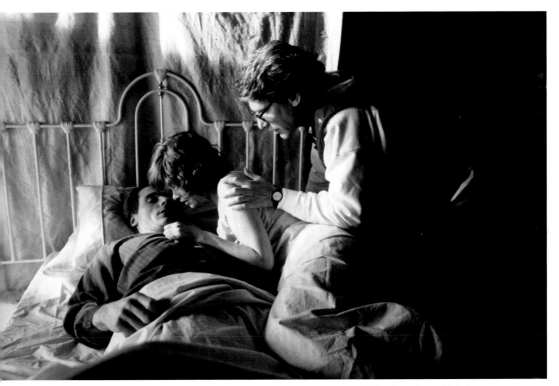

Jeremy Irons, Geneviève Bujold and David Cronenberg, *Dead Ringers*, 1988. Photo: Susan Meiselas

It seems incredible, but when one considers a talent like **Luis Buñuel**, the same epithets that some people use to accuse him of being unbearable are used by others to describe the very reasons for his success. For his detractors, Buñuel was a desecrator, blasphemous, iconoclastic and daring. And for the many people who have loved his work, he was admired precisely because of those things.

Born in Spain in 1900 (the same year that Freud's *Interpretation of Dreams* was published), Buñuel's childhood was spent in a Jesuit college, which left him with an indelible streak of fierce anti-clericalism. At university in Madrid, he studied literature and philosophy, and got to know Federico García Lorca, Salvador Dalí, Rafael Alberti and Ramón Gómez de la Serna. After graduation, he travelled to Paris to be near to the surrealists. His first film was *Un chien andalou* (An Andalusian Dog) (1928), a collaboration with Dalí. Two years later in *L'Âge d'or* (The Golden Age), he was already critical of the bourgeoisie and its 'discreet charm', and he subsequently demonstrated this distaste with all his force in one of his last and most famous films, *Le charme discret de la bourgeoisie* (The Discreet Charm of the Bourgeoisie) (1972).

Anti-bourgeois and anti-clerical, Buñuel tried in his films to break up the constructed order; the social relationships that bind us, the houses we live in, the families that we build, are based on a code made up of harsh and obsolete formulae, founded on an evil spell that, in essence, it would take very little to break apart. And in his films the strange, anachronistic and, indeed, 'surreal' conversations are, furthermore, slashes in the veil of our consciousness.

Of all his films, *Belle de jour* (The Daylight Beauty) (1967) is without doubt the most successful and Séverine, played by a dazzling Catherine Deneuve, lives for us on a plane of continuous double existence, between dream and reality.

Buñuel was fascinated by dreamlike states: 'Dreams are the first cinema invented by mankind, and they have a greater wealth of possibilities than cinema itself. Not even the richest producer could finance the superproduction of certain dreams. But we always talk about dreams and forget daydreams, *rêverie*. I think I prefer those to dreams because you can't direct dreams, but *rêverie*, you can.'

Overleaf: Roman Polanski, *Pirates,* 1985. Photo: Douglas Kirkland

Luis Buñuel (left) and Catherine Deneuve, *Belle de jour*, 1967. Photo: Album

Rita Hayworth photographs Burt Lancaster on the set of *The Unforgiven*, directed by John Huston, 1960.
Photo: Phil Stern/CPI

Alec Guinness, *The Bridge on the River Kwai*, directed by David Lean, 1957. Photo: Everett Collection

An old clown now afflicted by alcoholism. A youthful promise of entertainment. A potential comeback. A short-lived success on stage. A sudden death that leaves a bitter taste in the mouth. In how many films does one find this story line? Many, no doubt, but they include *Limelight* (1952), the last film that **Charlie Chaplin** made in the United States before seeking refuge in Europe to escape McCarthyite persecution (he only returned in 1972 to accept his honorary Oscar).

No one knows if photographer W. Eugene Smith, before accepting the job of stills photographer on set, already knew the story of the film, about the fortunes of the clown Calvero, and that Chaplin, the actor who played him, was being hounded by McCarthy. But it was certainly a story that was very much to his taste.

Smith was a great photographer and a man of unshakeably high principles. He was fascinated by the pursuit of freedom and justice, he was profoundly religious, and above all, he was deeply engaged in the destiny of man in general and his own destiny in particular – and he maintained his only real prejudice was a search for truth.

He had created photo-stories for *Life* magazine, which are still seen as milestones of documentary photography. He had worked in the Pacific during the Second World War, reporting on the heavy casualties. Shortly afterwards he threw himself into a magnificent utopian project, like many of Smith's endeavours, that of telling the story of a city, Pittsburgh, in photographs, fragmented into a thousand different images, a thousand different moments to be recorded, each one important and each one significant.

There are very few traces left, in the annals of photography at least, of this meeting between Smith, the most romantic, extreme, brilliant documentary photographer, and the great Charlie Chaplin. Only this photograph remains: the director-producer-author-actor-clown seated below his movie camera, about to whistle to attract his crew's attention. A man, who with his work, as Smith might have said, pursued truth at all costs.

Opposite: Charlie Chaplin, *Limelight*, 1952. Photo: W. Eugene Smith

PLAYING
ROLES

My whole career has been fulfilling my childhood fantasies, playing characters that are larger than life, getting to play a knight, an elf, a prince, and a soldier.

Orlando Bloom

Clark Gable, Spencer Tracy, Robert Taylor and William Powell at MGM Studios, 1936.
Photo: Everett Collection

There are actors and there are characters: there are faces and masks. And sometimes the mask overwhelms the face and becomes imprinted into the audience's memory with the power of a primary image. Nor should we forget that occasionally there are also actors who become their own masks, which lend them an unforgettable or unmistakable aspect: Toto, Stan and Ollie, Charlie Chaplin....
It is nearly always comic actors who are able to transform a feature of their body (a prominent jaw, an extra-large frame, a penguin-like way of walking) into a comic device and, at the same time, into a means of recognition, of identification. Perhaps by exaggerating, accentuating certain specific characteristics, they become easier to remember. It may be because of this that in cinema certain actors become 'character actors', identified with something that makes them immediately recognizable: an elderly smart aleck's way of talking (Walter Brennan), a know-it-all kid's impudent way of looking at you (Macaulay Culkin, at least until he became too grown up), the penetrating gaze of a woman who can see right through you (Françoise Rosay), or the polished manners of the perfect butler (Eugene Pallette). Sometimes it is an asset, sometimes it's a curse, but an actor can easily become typecast in the same sort of role.

A characterisation can also be something else: a state of mind, a moral attitude, or a choice of genre. In other words, a character can be built upon the acting that accentuates this or that specific feature and which helps the audience understand the forces at work.

Johnny Depp and Winona Ryder in *Edward Scissorhands*, directed by Tim Burton, 1990.
Photo: 20th Century Fox

In the early days, in what, for the sake of brevity can be called 'classic cinema', everything was much simpler and clearer. As Alan Bennett wrote in his unfailingly witty book, *Untold Stories*, when he talks about being an enthusiastic film-goer ('we went to the pictures at least twice a week'), he is able to decipher at once a character's true nature from his external appearance. If the character had well-brushed silver hair and wore a double-breasted overcoat, this meant that one had to be wary, because 'Bad men wear

Macaulay Culkin, 1994. Photo: 20th Century Fox

Theda Bara in *Cleopatra*, directed by J. Gordon Edwards, 1917. Photo: Everett Collection

Burt Lancaster in *The Crimson Pirate*, directed by Robert Siodmak, 1952. Photo: Everett Collection

Ewan McGregor in *Star Wars: Episode II – Attack of the Clones*, dir. George Lucas, 2002. Photo: Lucasfilm

good suits; honest men wear raincoats, and so untiring are they in the pursuit of evil that they sometimes forget to shave.' Clothes were very much part of the rules of acting and behaviour.

Things are a little different today. Directors enjoy mixing up these elements deliberately, creating ambiguities and unexpected reversals in their characters to surprise the audience. But this doesn't really change things so very much. It remains the task of the character to fix him or herself into the audience's imagination and make the film that they are watching unforgettable.

P.M.

ADVENTURERS

Should we have fewer of them? If we are truly honest, then the answer is no! Without them, films would have no flavour, they would lack relish. Adventurers are essential ingredients in any self-respecting story. Certainly, in the end we are happy if goodness and justice triumph, if love overcomes all obstacles, if peace follows victory, but in order to get there we need to feel a little adrenaline flowing through our veins, to feel a shiver running down our spines. Otherwise, it can all get just a little boring! And who better than a rogue to make sure that a film will have unexpected twists, and some inevitable low blows? Sometimes, it's enough for a character to have an air of ambiguity, or even a dark side, as when Clint Eastwood plays Dirty Harry. Other times, the role becomes intertwined perfectly with a particular way of smiling, of emphasizing an ironic allusion (as perfected by Steve McQueen in *Bullitt*). Or their defining moments can be the situations that force characters to behave in unorthodox ways, making it easier to resort to some surprising tricks, such as those which Tyrone Power's Zorro, Burt Lancaster's Crimson Pirate, or Harrison Ford's Indiana Jones were capable of. The adventurer knows that they will always have the sympathy of the audience, who are ever ready to forgive them for even the most heinous of crimes.

Jeff Bridges in *True Grit*, directed by Ethan and Joel Coen, 2010. Photo: Wilson Webb

Errol Flynn in *The Adventures of Robin Hood*, directed by Michael Curtiz, 1938. Photo: Everett Collection

Rudolph Valentino in *The Four Horsemen of the Apocalypse*, dir. Rex Ingram, 1921. Photo: John Kobal Foundation

Tyrone Power in *The Mark of Zorro*, directed by Rouben Mamoulian, 1940. Photo: Everett Collection

Douglas Fairbanks Jr. in *Sinbad the Sailor*, directed by Richard Wallace, 1947. Photo: John Kobal Foundation

David Niven in *Around the World in Eighty Days*, directed by Michael Anderson, 1956. Photo: David Seymour

Steve McQueen, James Coburn, Horst Buchholz, Yul Brynner, Brad Dexter, Robert Vaughn and Charles Bronson:
The Magnificent Seven, directed by John Sturges, 1960. Photo: Everett Collection

Johnny Depp in *Pirates of the Caribbean: Dead Man's Chest*, dir. Gore Verbinski, 2006. Photo: Walt Disney Co.

Katharine Ross, Robert Redford, Paul Newman in *Butch Cassidy*, dir. George Roy Hill, 1969. Photo: 20th Century Fox

Albert Finney in *Tom Jones*, directed by Tony Richardson, 1963. Photo: Everett Collection

Keanu Reeves in *The Matrix Reloaded*, directed by Andy and Lana Wachowski, 2003. Photo: Album

Tom Cruise in *Mission: Impossible – Ghost Protocol*, directed by Brad Bird, 2011. Photo: Album

Overleaf: Harrison Ford in *Raiders of the Lost Ark*, directed by Steven Spielberg, 1981.
Photo: Everett Collection

BORN YESTERDAY

Naive, but never stupid; delicate, but not made of glass. Sometimes, as in *Amélie*, an unworldly character can seem to inhabit a fairy tale, can enchant us without falling into sugary clichés. The same is true in *Born Yesterday*, George Cukor's film that justly deserved the Oscar awarded to an irresistible Judy Holliday. She is the dizzy-headed girl who, in the end, is nonetheless able to draw on all the wit and strength necessary to rebel against her truly thick-headed male exploiter. Beautiful, but no femme fatale, rather a more ethereal being, often ironic and elegant, like the unforgettable Audrey Hepburn, or an impeccable and smiling wife, like Doris Day. Many women identified with them, and many men were inevitably enchanted forever after. It goes without saying that these poor naive creatures have to suffer a little in love, and this is typified by the misadventures of Bridget Jones – who is so likeable, after all, because she is so 'normal'. A thirty-something singleton, an ordinary woman, who frets about her weight, who feels bad because she smokes and drinks too much, is worried about her disastrous relationships with the opposite sex, and is constantly searching for her ideal man. In the end, however, all the awkward spontaneity of characters like Bridget cannot but be recognized and rewarded with a guaranteed happy ending.

Audrey Tautou in *Amélie*, directed by Jean-Pierre Jeunet, 2001. Photo: Eyevine

June Allison, 1946. Photo: Everett Collection

Doris Day, 1948. Photo: Album

Ginger Rogers, 1947. Photo: Everett Collection

Paulette Goddard, 1936. Photo: Everett Collection

Jean Simmons in *Hamlet*, directed by Laurence Olivier, 1948. Photo: Album

Romy Schneider in *Sissi*, directed by Ernst Marischka, 1955. Photo: Album

Maureen O'Sullivan in *Tarzan the Ape Man*, directed by W.S. Van Dyke, 1932. Photo: Everett Collection

Judy Holliday in *Born Yesterday*, directed by George Cukor, 1950. Photo: Album

Winona Ryder in *The Age of Innocence*, directed by
Martin Scorsese, 1993. Photo: Columbia Pictures

Claire Danes in *Romeo + Juliet*, directed by
Baz Luhrmann, 1996. Photo: 20th Century Fox

Renée Zellweger in *Bridget Jones: The Edge of Reason*,
directed by Beeban Kidron, 2004. Photo: Universal

Anne Hathaway in *The Princess Diaries 2*, directed
by Garry Marshall, 2004. Photo: Buena Vista

Audrey Hepburn, 1955. Photo: Philippe Halsman

Overleaf: Jessica Lange in *King Kong*, directed by John Guillermin, 1976.
Photo: Everett Collection

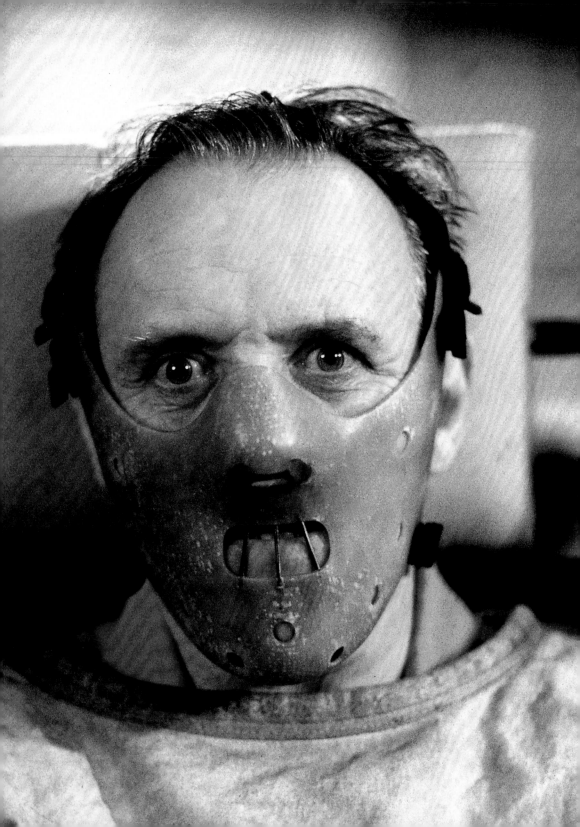

VAMPIRES AND MONSTERS

So pale and yet so elegant; so seductive and yet so ravenous. From Bela Lugosi's Dracula to Robert Pattinson's Edward Cullen, the lead in the *Twilight* series, vampires occupy the top spot in the hierarchy of literary and cinematic monsters, which also includes orcs and werewolves, mutants and cannibals. But they are also implacable psychopaths and sharp-clawed avengers, able to rip through the delicate veil that separates dreams from reality. Women fear them, but there is an irresistible attraction to those hungry fangs, destined to leave their mark on defenceless snow-white flesh. Certainly, the gruesome versions of Nosferatu played by Max Schreck and Klaus Kinski, who are bald and stooping, do not do justice to the beauty and sensuality of Bram Stoker's creature. But woe betide anyone who lets themselves be deceived by appearances (even a peculiar, other-worldly hairstyle should be enough to arouse suspicion!). Behind the mask of perfect gentlemen like Hannibal Lecter, who love to have 'friends for dinner', lurk bloodthirsty beasts, just as Shrek's ugly exterior conceals the soul of a gentle and kindly ogre. It is up to the viewer to work out which is which.

Anthony Hopkins in *The Silence of the Lambs*, directed by Jonathan Demme, 1991. Photo: Orion Pictures

Robert Englund in *A Nightmare on Elm Street*, directed by Wes Craven, 1984. Photo: Album

Shrek and Puss in Boots in *Shrek 2*, directed by Andrew Adamson, Kelly Asbury and Conrad Vernon, 2004.
Photo: Album

Jack Nicholson in *The Shining*, directed by Stanley Kubrick, 1980. Photo: Warner Brothers

Javier Bardem in *No Country for Old Men*, directed by Ethan and Joel Coen, 2007. Photo: Album

Robert Pattinson in *New Moon*, directed by Chris Weitz, 2009.
Photo: David Strick

Christopher Lee in *Dracula*, directed by Terence Fisher,
1958. Photo: Everett Collection

Winona Ryder and Gary Oldman in *Bram Stoker's Dracula*,
dir. Francis Ford Coppola, 1992. Photo: Everett Collection

Bela Lugosi in *Mark of the Vampire*, directed by
Tod Browning, 1935. Photo: Clarence Sinclair Bull

Max Schreck in *Nosferatu*, directed by Wilhelm Murnau,
1922. Photo: Everett Collection

Ben Chapman in *Creature from the Black Lagoon*, directed by Jack Arnold, 1954. Photo: John Kobal Foundation

Marty Feldman in *Young Frankenstein*, directed by Mel Brooks, 1974. Photo: 20th Century Fox

CHILD STARS

It all began with Jackie Coogan, who started out as the cute kid at Charlie Chaplin's side and ended up playing Uncle Fester in the TV series *The Addams Family*. From Liz Taylor and Shirley Temple to Christina Ricci and Dakota Fanning, not to mention Enzo Staiola, Mickey Rooney, Jodie Foster, Drew Barrymore, Macaulay Culkin, Jean Pierre Leaud, Christian Bale, Leonardo DiCaprio and Natalie Portman, every era in the history of cinema has had its share of child prodigies. Some are blessed with lifelong success, while others are cursed by an unhappy adult life. If there is a child (or an animal for that matter) in a film, drawing all the attention, it is so much the worse for the superstar leads. It's every actor's worst nightmare, so they say, trying to redress the balance. One just has to think of the Volpi Cup for best actress awarded at the 1996 Venice Film Festival to the female lead of Jacques Doillon's *Ponette*. And what age was the winner? Just four years old! More than able to put any Hollywood star in the shade and to steal scenes from the most charismatic actors, it is the youngest performers who can effortlessly win over the public's heart and hold producers and the box-office in the palm of their hands.

Margaret O'Brien in *Jane Eyre*, directed by Robert Stevenson, 1943. Photo: Everett Collection

Natalie Portman in *Leon*, directed by Luc Besson, 1994. Photo: Columbia Pictures

Daniel Radcliffe in *Harry Potter and the Philosopher's Stone*, directed by Chris Columbus, 2001.
Photo: Warner Brothers

Elizabeth Taylor in *Courage of Lassie*, directed by Fred McLeod Wilcox, 1946. Photo: Everett Collection

Pablito Calvo in *Miracle of Marcelino*, directed by Ladislao Vajda, 1955. Photo: Album

Jackie Coogan in *The Kid*, directed by Charlie Chaplin, 1921. Photo: Everett Collection

Mickey Rooney, 1934. Photo: Everett Collection

Shirley Temple in *Baby Take a Bow*, directed by Harry Lachman, 1934. Photo: Everett Collection

Brooke Shields in *Pretty Baby*, directed by Louis Malle, 1978. Photo: Everett Collection

Asa Butterfield in *Hugo*, directed by Martin Scorsese, 2011.
Photo: Jaap Buitendijk

HEROES

'No one should go to the movies unless they believe in heroes,' said John Wayne, and it is hard to disagree. Warriors and cowboys, sheriffs and lawyers, policemen and soldiers, secret agents and outlaws, revolutionaries from history and post-apocalyptic avengers, officers and gentlemen: these characters travel over stormy seas, cross desolate prairies or walk through crowded city streets, and it is not hard to recognize them. They have broad shoulders and a proud look. They say things like 'I never killed a man who didn't deserve it' (the always tough John Wayne), or propose a romantic toast 'To ancient evenings and distant music' (Clint Eastwood). Some of them are cold, indestructible and unapproachable. Others are more rumpled, ready to show their wounds and weaknesses. Whether on a mission from God or for the people, the heroes of the big screen are solitary glamorous creatures, with rough manners and hard hearts. With a trademark move or catchphrase that never lets them down, the hero is transformed into an icon. Sometimes all it takes is an evening jacket and a martini, *et les jeux sont faits*.

Brad Pitt in *Troy*, directed by Wolfgang Petersen, 2004. Photo: Warner Brothers

Al Pacino in *Serpico*, directed by Sidney Lumet, 1973.
Photo: Everett Collection

Sidney Poitier in *In the Heat of the Night*, directed by
Norman Jewison, 1967. Photo: Dennis Stock

Denzel Washington in *Glory*, directed by Edward Zwick,
1990. Photo: Everett Collection

Gregory Peck in *To Kill a Mockingbird*, directed by
Robert Mulligan, 1962. Photo: Everett Collection

Mel Gibson in *Braveheart*, directed by Mel Gibson, 1995.
Photo: Eyevine

Kirk Douglas in *Paths of Glory*, directed by Stanley Kubrick, 1957. Photo: Everett Collection

Henry Fonda in *My Darling Clementine*, directed by John Ford, 1946. Photo: John Kobal Foundation

Russell Crowe in *Master and Commander*, directed by
Peter Weir, 2003. Photo: 20th Century Fox

Kevin Costner in *Dances with Wolves*, directed by
Kevin Costner, 1990. Photo: Orion Pictures

Tom Hanks in *Saving Private Ryan*, directed by
Steven Spielberg, 1998. Photo: DreamWorks

Kurt Russell in *Escape from New York*, directed by
John Carpenter, 1981. Photo: Avco Embassy

Uma Thurman in *Kill Bill: Vol. 1*, directed by Quentin Tarantino, 2003.
Photo: Miramax

Sigourney Weaver in
Aliens, directed by
James Cameron, 1986.
Photo: Douglas Kirkland

SUPERHEROES

First came the heroes: Zorro and Tarzan, then Sherlock Holmes and Conan the Barbarian. But when these 'ordinary' humans are not strong enough to change the destiny of a world gone mad, that's the moment the superhero makes an appearance: from Mandrake the Magician and the Phantom, to Flash Gordon, Superman, Batman and Wonder Woman. These mysterious beings with superhuman powers often conceal ancient sorrows and shameful secrets behind their masks and brightly coloured costumes: superheroes – especially those created by Marvel Comics – with super problems. Men with green skin or bodies of stone; women who can become cats or turn invisible. Strong, fast, clever, noble and courageous, they may live a solitary existence or be part of an unassailable team of different talents; their souls are split between a dull everyday life and breathtaking adventures. In the last hundred years they have fought world wars and battled for civil rights, and they are now seeing a revival on the big screen, as characters in a cinematic world that has become ever more immense.

George Clooney in *Batman & Robin*, directed by Joel Schumacher, 1997. Photo: Warner Brothers

Tobey Maguire in *Spider-Man 3*, directed by Sam Raimi, 2007. Photo: Sony Pictures

Christopher Reeve in *Superman*, directed by Richard Donner, 1978. Photo: Burt Glinn

Victor Mature in *Samson and Delilah*, directed by
Cecil B. DeMille, 1949. Photo: Everett Collection

Bartolomeo Pagano in *Cabiria*, directed by
Giovanni Pastrone, 1914. Photo: Everett Collection

Steve Reeves in *Il terrore dei barbari* (Goliath and the Barbarians), directed by Carlo Campogalliani, 1959.
Photo: Everett Collection

Arnold Schwarzenegger in *Conan the Destroyer*, directed by John Milius, 1984. Photo: Universal

Michelle Pfeiffer in *Batman Returns*, directed by Tim Burton, 1992.
Photo: Warner Brothers

Chris Evans, Michael Chiklis, Jessica Alba, Ioan Gruffudd:
Fantastic Four, dir. Tim Story, 2005. Photo: 20th Century Fox

Hugh Jackman in *X2*, directed by Bryan Singer, 2003.
Photo: 20th Century Fox

Chris O'Donnell in *Batman & Robin*, directed by
Joel Schumacher, 1997. Photo: Warner Brothers

Wesley Snipes in *Blade: Trinity*, directed by
David S. Goyer, 2004. Photo: New Line Cinema

FEMMES FATALES

Blood-red lips clamped around a cigarette, dynamite glances barely hidden by a flicker of the eyelashes, vermilion nails ready to seize their prey, plunging necklines and slit skirts. Femmes fatales were born with cinema itself (Theda Bara, the early silent film actress, is often considered to be the first) – seductresses exploding onto the screen and creeping into the fantasies of those who made the films as well as those who watched them. They are mysterious, dangerous and ultra-sensual. As Orson Welles says in *The Lady from Shanghai*, recalling his encounter with the peroxide blonde Rita Hayworth, 'If I'd known where it would end, I'd never let anything start, if I'd been in my right mind, that is. But once I'd seen her, once I'd seen her, I was not in my right mind for quite some time....' In film, femmes fatales have become the projection of male desires and fears, but they often embody the dreams of women, too. For, in truth, what woman would not like to see herself at least once assuming the role of Marlene Dietrich as Shanghai Lily or Uma Thurman as Mrs. Mia Wallace?

Uma Thurman in *Pulp Fiction*, directed by Quentin Tarantino, 1994. Photo: Miramax

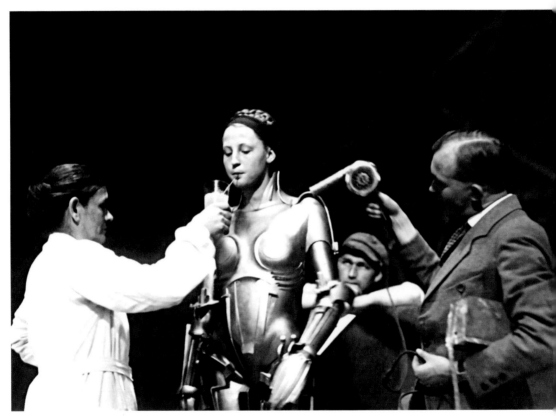

Brigitte Helm in *Metropolis*, directed by Fritz Lang, 1927. Photo: Everett Collection

Marlene Dietrich in *The Blue Angel*, directed by Josef von Sternberg, 1930. Photo: Everett Collection

Rita Hayworth in *Gilda*, directed by Charles Vidor, 1946.
Photo: Everett Collection

Veronica Lake, 1942. Photo: John Kobal Foundation

Jeanne Moreau in *Eva*, directed by Josef Losey, 1962.
Photo: Everett Collection

Mary Astor, 1935. Photo: Everett Collection

Barbara Stanwyck in *Double Indemnity*, directed by
Billy Wilder, 1944. Photo: Everett Collection

Sharon Stone in *Basic Instinct*, directed by Paul Verhoeven, 1992. Photo: Tristar Pictures

Isabella Rossellini in *Blue Velvet*, directed by David Lynch, 1986. Photo: De Laurentiis Group

Scarlett Johansson in *The Black Dahlia*, directed by
Brian De Palma, 2006. Photo: Universal

Glenn Close in *Fatal Attraction*, directed by
Adrian Lyne, 1987. Photo: Everett Collection

Kathleen Turner in *Body Heat*, directed by
Lawrence Kasdan, 1981. Photo: Everett Collection

Faye Dunaway in *Chinatown*, directed by
Roman Polanski, 1974. Photo: Everett Collection

Zhang Ziyi in *2046*, directed by Wong Kar-wai, 2004. Photo: Sony Pictures

CLOWNS

If cinema took its first steps at the circus and in county fairs, this was certainly no accident. It's where clowns are at home, and they still inspire dozens of characters today who, having left the big top far behind, penetrate the DNA of comic films. They are foreign bodies in the reality that surrounds them, eternal children always struggling against society and its ridiculous rules. The clown-like figures of the big screen, with roots in the two main traditional styles of clowning, auguste and whiteface, transform life into a circus arena; they personify all our anxieties and neuroses and expose the paradoxes of human existence, while hiding a tear behind a smile. 'I believe in the power of laughter and tears as an antidote to hatred and terror,' said Charlie Chaplin. From the gentle Little Tramp to the childlike Mr Bean, they are the awkward incarnation of the unimpressive little man. They share a feeling of inadequacy and hide their own discomfort under their ill-fitting clothes.

Robin Williams, 2002. Photo: Martin Schoeller

Buster Keaton in *The Navigator*, 1924. Photo: John Kobal Foundation

The Marx Brothers, 1935. Photo: Clarence Sinclair Bull

Stan Laurel and Oliver Hardy in *Swiss Miss*, directed by John G. Blystone, 1938.
Photo: Everett Collection

Fernandel, 1953. Photo: Philippe Halsman

Bob Hope, 1950. Photo: Philippe Halsman

Louis de Funès, 1976. Photo: Album

Totò in *Fifa e arena*, directed by Mario Mattoli, 1948.
Photo: AFE

Peter Sellers in *The Pink Panther*, directed by
Blake Edwards, 1963. Photo: Everett Collection

Giulietta Masina in *La strada*, directed by
Federico Fellini, 1954. Photo: Everett Collection

Goldie Hawn, 1979. Photo: CBS

John Cleese, 1970. Photo: Everett Collection

Eddie Murphy in *Coming to America*, directed by
John Landis, 1988. Photo: Paramount

Rowan Atkinson in *Johnny English*, directed by
Peter Howitt, 2003. Photo: Album

Ben Stiller in *Starsky & Hutch*, directed by
Todd Phillips, 2004. Photo: Album

John Belushi in *Animal House*, directed by
John Landis, 1978. Photo: Universal

Jim Carrey in *Ace Ventura: Pet Detective*, directed by Tom Shadyac, 1994. Photo: Warner Brothers

Dean Martin and Jerry Lewis, 1951. Photo: Philippe Halsman

Jacques Tati, 1954. Photo: Philippe Halsman

Charlie Chaplin has been accused of many things: engaging in anti-American activities, being a dangerous communist sympathizer, covering up his French-Jewish ancestry.

Rereading these accusations raised against the great English actor and director during the McCarthy era, or flicking through the FBI and MI5's dossiers, which are now accessible, it soon becomes clear that a defamatory and persecutory campaign was being conducted against the man who created the most brilliant mask in comedy, one constructed with comic wit and wisdom, and who also produced masterpieces such as *The Vagabond*, *City Lights*, *The Great Dictator* and *Limelight*. But yet, despite the lack of evidence, Chaplin's successes were not enough to keep this great entertainer in America and in 1952 what he had planned as a short trip to attend the London premiere of *Limelight* became the start of a very long exile.

But a great actor decides when he will leave the stage, and so before his departure Chaplin decided to say goodbye to his audience in an irreverent and bitter way by creating a special portrait. Richard Avedon recalled how he received a strange telephone call one day from someone claiming to be Charlie Chaplin who wanted to arrange a photo session at short notice. At first, the photographer thought that it was a practical joke, and only when the great actor insisted did Avedon understand that the person at the other end of the line was entirely serious. Chaplin arrived at Avedon's studio the next day and left again shortly afterwards. During a brief but intense encounter between actor and photographer, an extraordinary image was captured, one that is unique for the force and bitter irony of Chaplin's gesture and his smile. Looking at it today, after so many years, one has to ask how a whole country could have been so afraid of this little devil.

Charlie Chaplin, New York, 13 September 1952.
Photo: Richard Avedon © The Richard Avedon Foundation

THE
BODY

I speak two languages, Body and English.

Mae West

Human beings are divided into mind and body. The mind embraces all the nobler aspirations, like poetry and philosophy, but the body has all the fun.

Woody Allen

Vin Diesel, 2011. Photo: Art Streiber

Brad Pitt, 1998. Photo: Bruce Davidson

Marlon Brando in *A Streetcar Named Desire*, directed by Elia Kazan, 1950. Photo: John Engstead

'How can a guy climb trees, say "Me, Tarzan, you, Jane," and make a million? The public forgives my acting because they know I was an athlete. They know I wasn't make-believe.'

Johnny Weissmuller was no imposter, nor was he an actor perhaps in the fullest sense of the word, but he was certainly a great athlete, both agile and dynamic. This was the only way that he could have carried off the role of being an ape man able to conquer the jungle while wearing a leopard-skin loincloth, swinging from one vine to the next.

In the 1920s Weissmuller was one of the best swimmers in the world – he had won five Olympic gold medals as well as countless other national titles, and had broken many international records. But his name is forever associated with Tarzan and the twelve Tarzan films he starred in. We also think of him as the archetypal 'natural' man, whose chest is always on display as a symbol of physical strength and moral integrity, full of strong and genuine emotions that he is ready to show in the face of any adversity that may befall him, whether it be in a city full of skyscrapers or in a jungle recreated in the studio.

Weissmuller's powerful, manly posing has inspired numerous on-screen heroes who have imbued their muscles, sometimes barely able to flex inside their tight-fitting T-shirts, with the same magnetism and energy.

Overleaf: Hedy Lamarr in *Ecstasy*, directed by Gustav Machatý, 1933. Photo: GBB Archive

Johnny Weissmuller in *Tarzan the Ape Man*, 1932. Photo: George Hurrell

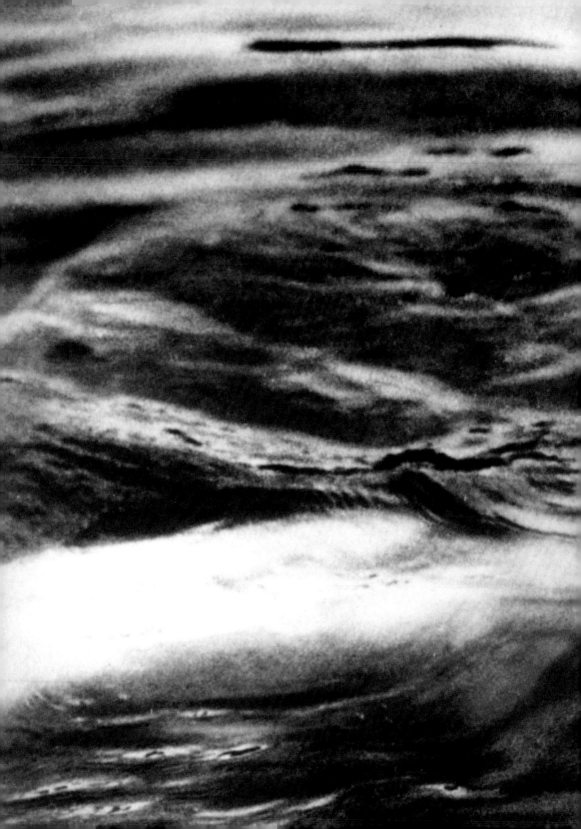

In *Picnic*, Hal Carter, played by **William Holden**, is a likeable drifter in dire straits who arrives one sweltering summer's day to disturb both the placid rhythms of a small town in America and the marriage plans laid by a social-climbing mother and her innocent daughter. With his handsome face, melancholy but sincere smile and muscular body, Holden, of course, gets the girl.

The career of this superb actor, which was marked by alcoholism and depression (and by a horrible incident in which he was guilty of causing a fatal car crash in Italy in the 1960s), is studded with films that are certainly more memorable than *Picnic*. One just has to think of *Sunset Boulevard* (1950), directed by Billy Wilder, which confirmed his status as a great actor; David Lean's epic *The Bridge on the River Kwai* (1957); the delicious *Sabrina* (1954), also directed by Billy Wilder, when he acted alongside Humphrey Bogart and Audrey Hepburn; or the mushily sentimental *Love Is a Many-Splendored Thing* (1955). All his most famous films are assured a place in the history of cinema. But it was his body, especially the burnished muscles that he displayed in *Picnic*, that made William Holden a sex symbol.

William Holden and Kim Novak in *Picnic*, directed by Joshua Logan, 1955. Photo: Everett Collection

Anita Ekberg in *La dolce vita*, directed by Federico Fellini, 1960. Photo: Pierluigi Praturlon

Sophia Loren in *Marriage Italian Style*, directed by Vittorio De Sica, 1964. Photo: Alfred Eisenstaedt

Sylvester Stallone's career is carved into his body, muscle by muscle. It's a career that has been far from easy, marked out by comebacks and stubbornness, of victories built on the daily grind of hard work.

Sylvester Gardenzio Stallone, born in 1946 in Hell's Kitchen, New York, had a difficult childhood as, amongst other things, his body was very fragile, almost too fragile for the life that awaited him. Infantile rickets exacerbated what appeared to be his total lack of interest at school (by the age of fifteen he had already been expelled from at least four schools) and moreover in society in general.

But it was the work he did on his body, building steadily over many years (as he practised fencing, American football and gymnastics) that made his fortune. He not only graduated from college, but won a study scholarship to the American College of Switzerland because of his sporting prowess. Sport helped him overcome his physical problems and the scholarship gave him the chance to enrol at the University of Miami in Florida, where he chose to study drama.

In this image of contrasts, it's as if the whole of the life of the actor who played both Rocky and Rambo, a life that began with such physical frailty, is encompassed. His muscles are tensed, but the delicately placed flower petals suggest a long-awaited moment of peace.

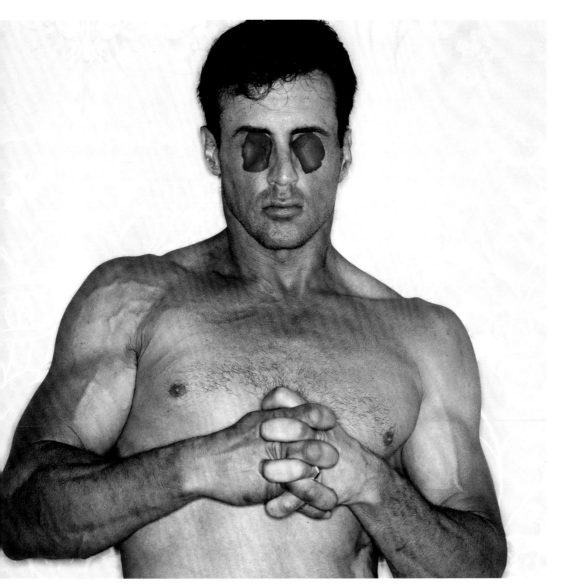

Sylvester Stallone, 1993. Photo: Michel Comte

Julia Roberts, 1990. Photo: Herb Ritts

Nicole Kidman, 1999. Photo: Herb Ritts

It's a well-known story now: it was 1978 and a group of young folk left Los Angeles for a tour of the desert. Amongst them was a photographer just beginning his career and a virtually unknown actor.

The car stopped at a service station and, as the desert light seemed to be so much part of this day of freedom, the photographer suggested to the actor that they should take some posed shots.

The photographer in question was Herb Ritts, a young man who had rejected a safe career in the family firm (selling expensive designer furniture in their store in Brentwood, Los Angeles). He was as fascinated by the modern portraitists as he was by the perfect images, compositions, use of light and materials of the European tradition. He very soon became, in fact, one of the most famous fashion and portrait photographers.

The actor was **Richard Gere**, and because the photographs were published in influential magazines they helped him to obtain major roles and to create the myth of a new 'angry' sex symbol.

'I put him in a pose that Paul Strand might have used with one of his models,' said Ritts, years later, as he recalled the improvised photo shoot in the desert. The choice of a frontal posture, the relationship between subject and setting, and Gere's direct stare into the camera may well place this image within the tradition of classic American portraiture, but there is no doubt that in Ritts's photographs, Richard Gere's body speaks in a highly explicit way that does not occur in Strand's images. The movement of his legs, the position of his arms, the muscles of his chest that bulge through his T-shirt: each element speaks of the strength, vitality and unabashed freedom of this young man who by his stare tells us that he is ready to do whatever it takes to succeed.

Richard Gere, 1979. Photo: Herb Ritts

Arnold Schwarzenegger, 1977. Photo: Elliott Erwitt

Arnold Schwarzenegger, 1977. Photo: Elliott Erwitt

Eve Arnold was born in 1913 in America into a family of Jewish Russian immigrants. Photography came into her life by chance. She was married, a mother and a working woman. But she took just one intense course of lessons with Alexey Brodovitch, the legendary art director of *Harper's Bazaar*, and that was all needed for photography to become her life, her profession.

She became a member of Magnum Photos, and it is said that Robert Capa, when seeing her photographs, described them as being 'halfway between Marlene Dietrich's legs and the bitter lives of potato pickers.' Beyond the hyperbole, all through her career Eve Arnold constantly moved between social reportage and glamour portraits, paying particular attention to women that Hollywood had immortalized on the screen and in print media. She sought to examine and understand how the glamour, constantly on show, was inevitably an unachievable model for the general public.

Eve Arnold often worked with **Marilyn Monroe** and a solid and affectionate relationship grew between them over time. In Arnold's portraits, Marilyn sometimes appears compliant, sometimes quite helpless, and at other times ready to play a game of seduction with her friend on the other side of the lens. 'She loved the camera,' Arnold said of her. 'And she loved doing studio work. I don't like that kind of photo, but I wanted to support her and I was curious to know what fantasies she had about herself. How would you like to appear? I asked her. What do you want to look like? And she said the Botticelli Venus…. We laughed a lot, I remember, especially towards the end when it was clear that, despite having sealed off the space we'd been working in with paper shades so as not to be disturbed by the men in the crew, they had managed to make a number of spyholes through which, for the whole afternoon, they had been watching us, gazing on with approval. She, of course, was well aware of this and she had been performing for them. While she was making love to my camera, in reality she was playing with them.'

Marilyn Monroe, 1960. Photo: Eve Arnold

Jane Fonda, 1970s. Photo: Just Jaeckin

Brigitte Bardot, 1951. Photo: Philippe Halsman

Shirley Eaton in *Goldfinger*, directed by Guy Hamilton, 1986. Photo: Eyevine

Kim Basinger in *9 1/2 Weeks*, directed by Adrian Lyne, 1986. Photo: MGM

Ursula Andress in *Dr. No*, directed by Terence Young, 1962. Photo: Everett Collection

Demi Moore in *Striptease*, directed by Andrew Bergman, 1996. Photo: Columbia Pictures

'If she'd ever had an eyelift, she'd have lost that famous look of hers,' said the photographer Peter Lindbergh. **Charlotte Rampling**'s slim figure, emblematic of a vibrant fragility, seemed unique on the screen. But without doubt behind that gaze, those penetrating eyes, there lies the secret of an enigma that has never been fully understood, of a life that's been complicated and, at times, painful, and of a multifaceted personality belonging to someone who is ready to throw herself fearlessly into new adventures.

As Luchino Visconti said when he persuaded Rampling to play the part of a woman much older and much more experienced than herself in *The Damned*, every age is hidden behind those eyes.

She is an incredibly versatile actress, playing every possible role that an actor could, or would, want to play. From the science fiction tale *Zardoz* with Sean Connery; to the femme fatale alongside Robert Mitchum (*Farewell, My Lovely*); to being the haunting memory of Woody Allen's ex-girlfriend (*Stardust Memories*);

to playing grotesque (*Max, Mon Amour*), dramatic (*The Verdict*), dark and sensual characters (*Angel Heart*).

Certainly amongst all these different roles her most controversial, the one that has been seared into our memories, is the one she played for Liliana Cavani in *The Night Porter* (1974). A young Jewish woman, Lucia Atherton, is a prisoner in a concentration camp who begins a sadomasochistic relationship with her tormentor, an astonishing Dirk Bogarde, and who bare-breasted, wearing long braces over her thin ribs and an SS peaked cap on her head, sings '*Wenn ich mir was wünschen dürfte*' ('If I could only wish myself something') for her malign lover.

A female body had never been used in this way in cinema, mixing sensuality and horror in such a superb fashion. Commenting on these scenes, Charlotte Rampling recalled how '*The New York Times* wrote that I had a sick brain…and I too, when I really think about the horror that I was embodying, feel awful. But controversial roles are the most interesting.'

Overleaf: Silvana Mangano in *Bitter Rice*, directed by Giuseppe De Santis, 1948. Photo: Augusto Di Giovanni

Charlotte Rampling in *The Night Porter*, directed by Liliana Cavani, 1974. Photo: Mario Tursi

Klaus Kinski in *L'important c'est d'aimer* (That Most Important Thing: Love), directed by Andrzej Zulawski, 1974. Photo: Jean Gaumy

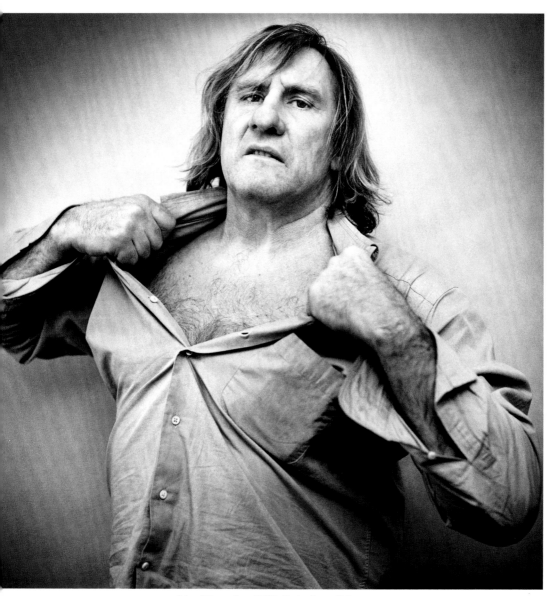

Gérard Depardieu, 2010. Photo: Serge Cohen

PRIVATE
LIVES

Being a movie star, and this applies to all of them, means being looked at from every possible direction. You are never left at peace, you're just fair game.

Greta Garbo

Anita Ekberg, 1953. Photo: © Phil Stern

'**M**ore stars than there are in heaven,' was Metro-Goldwyn-Mayer's motto. But the stars didn't just fill the studios, they also lived in the hills around Los Angeles. And if the life that they pretended to live on screen had great peaks of heroism, passion and good feeling, things could turn out quite differently in the real lives taking place behind the closed doors of Hollywood.

Occultist Aleister Crowley summed up the place concisely as 'an oasis of drug-addled sex fanatics', and Hollywood in its golden years was a unending party for Chaplin and Valentino, Erich von Stroheim and Robert Mitchum, Lana Turner and Judy Garland – the list could go on and on.

It would have mattered very little what was going on in private if the people involved were not film stars, but public life, the verisimilitude on the screen, was never enough (it is still not enough, to judge from the numbers of gossip magazines that are produced and sold around the world). It seems to be characteristic of the star system itself that it appropriates in an almost compulsive way anything that belongs to the personalities that populate it. Everything becomes part of the scene, everything is entertainment, every tiny little glitter of the star, even when it is something deeply private or murky and unsavoury.

The famous union, which Kenneth Anger also adopted as the title of his successful book *Hollywood Babylon*, between golden-era film-land and the Biblical cradle of perdition, bears witness

Sienna Miller and Cameron Diaz with friends at a party in Hollywood, 2007. Photo: Mark Petersen

to those continuous incursions, that blending of images between the public arena and life behind the scenes.

It was Kenneth Anger's book (a chronicle of the everyday goings-on in the mecca of cinema) that brought to light this hidden aspect of the double life of the stars, such perfect gentlemen or ladies on the screen, but in real life fragile mixed-up beings at the mercy of their own emotional instabilities. In *Hollywood Babylon* the actors appear as capricious, but intensely human divinities (and there are similarities with the Gods of Olympus), who can never curb their appetites, no matter how vile or horrible they might be. The final result is a gossipy, hallucinatory story that does not detract from but, above all, emphasizes, if that's at all possible, the highlights and lowlights of Hollywood personalities.

Norma Shearer and her husband, producer Irving Thalberg, 1931. Photo: Everett Collection

Dennis Hopper with Jack Nicholson at a Los Angeles Lakers game, 2004. Photo: Vince Bucci

However, this process of revelation and damnation only serves to enhance the legend. The myths feed themselves on an endless stream of base behaviour, scandals experienced and perpetrated, arrests and voracious sexual appetites, bisexuality and homosexuality. The legends extended from everyday abuses (for which Joan Crawford's disputed biography, written by her adopted daughter Christina, is a perfect example) all the way to homicide (one of the most sensational scandals involved Lana Turner and the 'mystery' – it was said – of the death of her lover, Johnny Stompanato, which had occurred during a night of arguments and passion at her Hollywood home.)

Not all Hollywood stars are tarnished by crimes and misdemeanours. But no matter how innocent or criminal their behaviour may be, the gossip merchants feed above all on their private lives. And if the tales push the limits of legality, or are simply too banal, what could be better than simply making up the gossip? Despite appearances, the film industry is full of tender-hearted mother figures who take care of the brood, of fathers who concentrate on swinging on the seesaw just to make their children happy. And couples who are apparently as carefree and happy as they are on screen, if not even happier.

It is important to always feed the myth, if the stars are to keep shining brightly. And even the dark side, the shadowy aspects of private lives (which can be straightforward, terrible, tragic and even genuinely peculiar) can help to keep the legend alive.

A.M.

They called him The Duke, and his career was bound up with the Western, from his very first film, *The Big Trail* (1930) to his last, *The Shootist* (1976). **John Wayne**'s career unfolded between these two titles, and was distinguished by his strong links to John Ford, with whom he made his most famous films, including *Stagecoach* (1939), the Western that was the turning point of his career; *Fort Apache* (1948); *She Wore a Yellow Ribbon* (1949); and *Rio Bravo* (1950). The myth of the rough-mannered man, good-hearted but chauvinistic and fundamentally reactionary, and never without his Stetson to shelter him from the fierce sun of Monument Valley, was born with these films.

The career of Phil Stern, a photographer from New York who soon found himself in Hollywood, was always connected with film productions. Stern took many of the classic photographs that tell the story of American cinema and its performers, from James Dean to Marilyn Monroe, Anita Ekberg and Frank Sinatra. Sincerely committed to democratic politics, and always in the front line at trade union disputes, Stern never hid his sympathies with the left.

That two such different personalities could become friends is still a mystery. Each time they met they never lost an opportunity to needle one another about their different political views, even insulting each other in jest. Yet, the bond between them was strong and their admiration reciprocal. Wayne allowed Stern privileged access to his private life, such as he gave to few others. In this image, even on a day off John Wayne still seems to be scanning the horizon, never to be parted from his Stetson.

John Wayne in Acapulco, 1940s. Photo: Phil Stern/CPI

Humphrey Bogart and his daughter Leslie, mid-1950s. Photo: Phil Stern/CPI

Audrey Hepburn and Mel Ferrer, 1960. Photo: Phil Stern/CPI

Jack Lemmon with his son Chris, 1955. Photo: Phil Stern/CPI

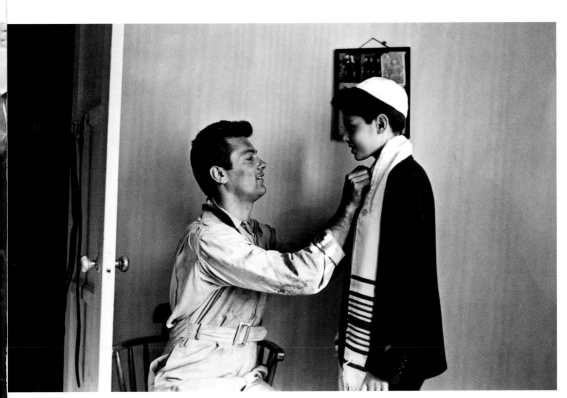

Tony Curtis with his brother Robert, 1953. Photo: Phil Stern/CPI

Agnès Varda and Jacques Demy at their home in Normandy, 1965. Photo: Pierre Boulat

Alfred Hitchcock's wife Alma, 1974. Photo: Philippe Halsman

Ingrid Bergman with her twins Isabella and Isotta, her daughters by Roberto Rossellini, 1952.
Photo: David Seymour

Elizabeth Taylor with her children, visiting Richard Burton on set, 1963. Photo: Eve Arnold

Paul Newman with his wife Joanne Woodward at their home in Westport, Connecticut, 1965. Photo: Bruce Davidson

Steve McQueen and his wife, 1963. Photo: John Dominis

It was Robert Capa who decided what path **Dennis Stock** would take. At the helm of the agency he himself had founded, Magnum Photos, Capa decided the destiny of young photographers according to the demands of the editorial market and of the agency that, in the 1950s, did its best to control that market.

And for Dennis Stock, the path led to Hollywood. Magnum did not have a correspondent in the mecca of cinema and Capa knew quite well (as he too felt the pull of the world of celluloid) how important it was not to neglect the private and public lives of the celebrities that filled the pages of glossy magazines.

Stock didn't take long to acclimatize himself and stayed in California for a long time, alternating between glamorous reportage and other more intense and personal projects, following – as he became more confident in the 1960s – the new alternative communities, the hippy movement, and the bikers who were seeking in their more or less haphazard fashion a different way of living.

But in Hollywood, Stock also managed to form some true friendships, like the one with a brilliant young actor, a genuine talent, who had a slightly introverted personality and was sadly destined to live a life that was all too short: James Dean.

They got to know one another in 1955 at a party, through a group of friends. They clicked at once and Dean invited him to a screening of *East of Eden* (1955), his first film. Together they decided to create a reportage, which would be like a visual on-the-road diary, retracing the actor's brief history in the places dear to his heart, from the State of Indiana where Dean was born in 1931, to New York City where he had begun his career as a theatre actor, and finally returning to California. The visual biography produced by Stock included extraordinary images, which, with the passage of time and the tragedy of Dean's death, have become even more emblematic. In this photograph Dean shivers with cold as he walks through Times Square in New York under the gaze of his friend.

James Dean in Times Square, New York, 1955. Photo: Dennis Stock

Vanessa Redgrave with her daughters Natasha and Joely, 1960s. Photo: Yul Brynner

Overleaf: Robert Redford, *c*. 1980. Photo: Douglas Kirkland

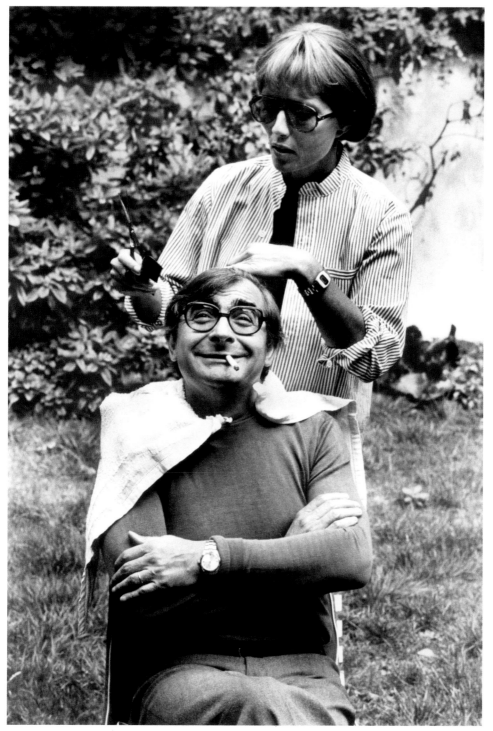

Claude Chabrol and his wife Stéphane Audran, 1976. Photo: Pierre Boulat

Romy Schneider and Alain Delon, 1959. Photo: Nicolas Tikhomiroff

Jane Fonda and Roger Vadim with the director's daughters, 1967. Photo: David Hurn

Everyone knows that he is the most famous war photographer in the world, the man who ushered in an era – still flourishing– of active photojournalism, which requires that one must be as close to the action as possible in order to capture it in the best possible way. And **Robert Capa** was certainly all that, but he was also a man who loved life's pleasures, enjoying games and grand drinking sessions in the company of friends.

The Second World War saw Capa travelling between different fronts and documenting a London stunned by the Blitz (1941); the North African campaign (1943); the advance of American troops through Italy, from Sicily to Rome; the Normandy beachhead (1943) and finally the liberation of France and Germany.

But whenever he could, as he became tired of war, Capa would take a break, and seek out photo assignments that were less demanding and lighter in tone, even undertaking some in well-known holiday destinations and catching up with his friends at the same time. His greatest friend of all was Ernest Hemingway, whom he photographed over the years in various different situations (while writing in his pyjamas, or hitting the bottle, during a hunt, or even in a hospital bed with a bandaged head after a banal, but nonetheless incredible car crash).

In October 1941 Hemingway was in Sun Valley, Idaho, where he was working on a film adaption of his *For Whom the Bell Tolls*. And there, amongst the mountains and quiet streams, Capa took this action shot of Gary Cooper who, with fishing rod in hand, is not going into battle but simply looking to catch some trout.

It seems like an idyllic moment of peace before they all return, in fiction and in real life, to the front line.

Overleaf: Charlize Theron, 2009. Photo: Emanuele Scorcelletti

Gary Cooper in Sun Valley, Idaho, 1941. Photo: Robert Capa

Yves Montand,
Simone Signoret,
Marilyn Monroe and
Arthur Miller, 1960.
Photo: Bruce Davidson

Nanni Moretti, 1994. Photo: Harry Gruyaert

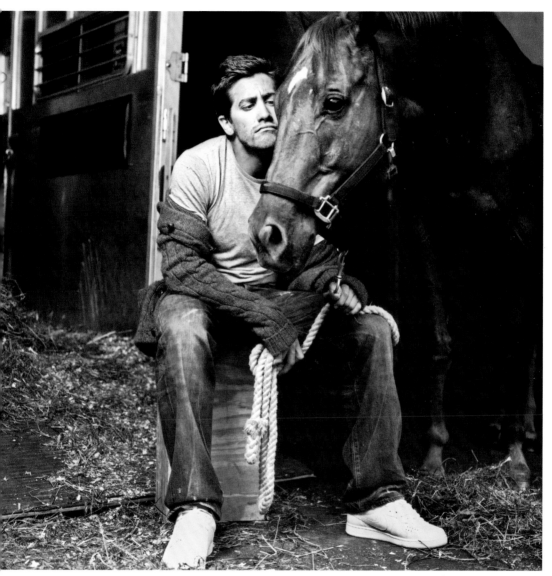

Jake Gyllenhaal, 2005. Photo: Martin Schoeller

Kate Winslet was the youngest actress ever to have received two Oscar nominations. She is a performer with a strong character and unusually, after her enormous global success in *Titanic*, she has chosen to refuse roles in big budget mega-productions, such as *Anna and the King* or *Shakespeare in Love*. She has instead dedicated herself to independent productions, and to difficult roles in low-budget films like *Hideous Kinky* (1998), directed by Gillies MacKinnon, or to intellectual roles as in *Holy Smoke* (1999), directed by Jane Campion.

And when it was suggested to documentary photographer **Paolo Pellegrin**, pride of Magnum Photos and notorious for his hard and precise style, that he should follow the Oscar candidates, Kate Winslet was obviously his first choice.

Paolo shadowed her, insinuating himself into the backstage of her everyday life, and photographed her while she prepared to confront her public on the evening of the Oscar ceremony. Pellegrin's style does not make any concessions, and instead of treating the occasion like a celebrity shoot at a luxury hotel (which essentially it was), he investigated his subject just as he would in his photojournalist work. But Winslet was happy to play along: her gaze is intense, concentrated and resolute. It is the gaze of someone who knows what's expected of them. She is preparing herself as any woman would before engaging with her work, consciously manipulating the instruments of her craft with an elegant professionalism. In this case, the instruments are her public image, her personality. A few months after this photo was taken, Winslet walked onto the stage of the Kodak Theater and, as predicted, received an Academy Award for her truly memorable performance in *The Reader*.

Kate Winslet, 2009. Photo: Paolo Pellegrin

Mickey Rourke, 2009. Photo: Paolo Pellegrin

Colin Farrell, 2011. Photo: Martin Schoeller

THE
PUBLIC EYE

If you're going to be a star, you have to look like a star, and I never go out unless I look like Joan Crawford the movie star. If you want to see the girl next door, go next door.

Joan Crawford

Penélope Cruz, Jeremy Irons and Renée Zellweger at the Oscars, 2005. Photo: Art Streiber

Marilyn Monroe and Jane Russell
at Grauman's Chinese Theatre,
Hollywood, 1953.
Photo: Everett Collection

Charlize Theron, 2004. Photo: Gary Hershorn

Julia Roberts, 2001. Photo: Gary Hershorn

Sandra Bullock, 2010. Photo: Gary Hershorn

Nicole Kidman, 2003. Photo: Mike Blake

Gwyneth Paltrow, 1999. Photo: Timothy A. Clary

Sandy Powell, 2010. Photo: Gary Hershorn

Hilary Swank, 2005. Photo: Gary Hershorn

Melissa Leo, 2011. Photo: Gary Hershorn

Lars von Trier at the Cannes Festival, 2011. Photo: Eric Gaillard

Previous pages: Dustin Hoffman, Clint Eastwood and Barbra Streisand, at the Oscars, 2005.
Photo: Art Streiber

Roberto Benigni celebrates winning an Oscar for *Life Is Beautiful*, 1999.
Photo: Eric Draper

Emmanuelle Béart at the Cannes Festival, 2006. Photo: Emanuele Scorcelletti

Bruce Willis at the Cannes Festival, 2006. Photo: Emanuele Scorcelletti

Cole Porter, Audrey Hepburn, Irving Berlin and a friend, 1950s. Photo: Phil Stern/CPI

Lauren Bacall, Humphrey Bogart and Rocky Cooper, mid-1950s. Photo: Phil Stern/CPI

Sidney Poitier, Susan Strasberg, Stanley Kramer and George Stevens Jr. at the Moscow Film Festival, 1967.
Photo: Phil Stern/CPI

MAGIC AND MAKE-BELIEVE

I think cinema, movies and magic have always been closely associated. The very earliest people who made films were magicians.

Francis Ford Coppola

Avatar, directed by James Cameron, 2009. Photo: 20th Century Fox

The Lord of the Rings: The Return of the King,
dir. Peter Jackson, 2003. Photo: New Line Cinema

There is a magical scene in *Singin'
in the Rain* that taps into one of
the secrets of the lure of cinema:
the capacity to create wonderful
fascinating worlds to which you
can travel in your mind and your heart.
It is about halfway through the film: Don
Lockwood (played by Gene Kelly) and
Kathy Selden (Debbie Reynolds) have
stopped fighting with one another, as they
have already realized that they have fallen
in love. Then Don, in order to explain his
work to her (he is a famous actor, and
she is a chorus girl), takes her into a vast
darkened studio. With a few well-chosen
lights, a little dry ice, a fan to make her
hair move as if in a spring breeze, the
whole scene changes around them; she is
no longer standing on a staircase but on a
balcony, the empty hangar has become a
magnificent panorama illuminated by the
pink light of a sunset, and he can sing with
all his heart *You Were Meant for Me*....

There may be no simpler, more direct
way of showing the film-goer how it is
possible to create whole worlds and
even universes from nothing (or virtually
nothing). Surely this is the key to the
mysteries of an art that has always played
hide and seek with reality: chasing it,
imitating it, but also challenging it, hiding
it, disguising it, and, finally, inventing it.

The real challenge for every true
director is to create alternative worlds,
be it the Kingdom of Carpathia or the
dark side of the Moon, the empire of
Captain Nemo or Snow White's enchanted
forest. Statistics and classifications are
meaningless if the public finds it more
beautiful to walk the streets of New York or
along the trails through Monument Valley

than to travel into the veins of the human
body or through Alice's magical looking
glass. There is no greater thrill than the
invention from nothing of a world that
does not exist, and making it welcoming
or hostile according to our fantasies.

The first film in the history of cinema
(or, more precisely, the one that was
screened for the first time in a cinema
selling tickets) brought reality to the screen
with the arrival of a train into a station,
and in such a believable and impressive
way that some of the spectators felt
compelled to leap out of their seats and
run out of the building. But not long
afterwards, beginning with Georges Méliès,
magic made its entrance into cinema and
realism was put to the side. Or perhaps
reality was modified, transformed and
magnified: a gamble that has not yet come
to an end and takes another step forward
with every innovation.

There are slightly more than seventy
years between Cooper and Schoedsack's
King Kong and Peter Jackson's remake
(by way of Guillermin). The actual story
hasn't changed much; the difference, for
today's film-goers, is the attention and
precision involved in the construction
of the prehistoric land of Skull Island.
Peter Jackson reflected that 'No film has

The Chronicles of Narnia, directed by
Andrew Adamson, 2005. Photo: Walt Disney Co.

Jordan Fry in *Charlie and the Chocolate Factory*,
dir. Tim Burton, 2005. Photo: Warner Brothers

The Neverending Story II, directed by
George Miller, 1990. Photo: Warner Brothers

captivated my imagination more than
King Kong. I'm making movies today
because I saw this film when I was 9
years old. It has been my sustained
dream to reinterpret this classic story for a
new age.' One can sense the pleasure of
giving a definite and solid form to a world
that no one has ever seen. The same
psychological mechanism lies behind
Jurassic Park (and all its imitators);
we can no longer be content with a
perfunctory and generic reconstruction,
we want perfection in every detail. This
is the ever more insistent demand that
we make of cinema.

P.M.

Intolerance, directed by
D.W. Griffith, 1916.
Photo: Album

Fantastic Voyage, directed by Richard Fleischer, 1966. Photo: 20th Century Fox

Keir Dullea in *2001: A Space Odyssey*, directed by Stanley Kubrick, 1968. Photo: Dmitri Kessel

Judy Garland in *The Wizard of Oz*,
directed by Victor Fleming, 1939.
Photo: Everett Collection

Of all the horrors, of all the monsters that have passed across the screen from cinema's beginnings until today, he is most definitely still the king.

King Kong's first appearance was in 1933, when directors Merian C. Cooper and Ernest B. Schoedsack conceived the story for the big screen, creating Skull Island, where the native people venerated Kong and tried to offer him a sacrifice in the form of the unwitting, blonde, beautiful actress Ann from New York.

We know the story: the terrifying giant ape has a gentle heart and falls in love with Ann, and not only does he spare her from his fury but he saves her from a series of dangers. Even when he is transported to New York in chains and is exposed to public derision, he still tries in vain to recover his beautiful Ann, until he is finally killed for having loved too much.

With a few variations on the theme, the story of King Kong has always remained more or less the same in its various different remakes, in 1962, in 1976 and 2005. And with each new adventure, new special effects (perhaps the most memorable are those created by Rambaldi for the version in 1976) have tried to trigger new visions and play with new variations on the theme of beauty and the beast.

King Kong, directed by Merian C. Cooper and Ernest B. Schoedsack, 1933. Photo: Ernest Bachrach

Johnny Depp in *Alice in Wonderland*, directed by Tim Burton, 2010. Photo: Walt Disney Co.

'I am a great liar. For me the things that are most true are the ones that I have invented myself. I am constantly faking things. I make a fake sea, a fake meadow, a fake thunderstorm. All this falsification, this representation – perhaps unconsciously – is simply the repetition of a kind of magic ritual.'

The sets that **Federico Fellini** created in the Cinecittà Studios in Rome are legendary. In those vast buildings his dreamlike worlds could come to life; the city of Rome, for example, became 'his' Rome, more real than the real thing. The Rimini of his childhood acquired a vitality that had the flavour of fond memories, as in the film *Amarcord* (1973). The appearance out at sea (an obviously pretend sea) of a transatlantic liner as it passes through the night along the Adriatic Coast, just a few miles from Rimini, prompts all the townsfolk to sail out in their little boats to greet the great ship.

'In the studio everything is fake, just like in real life, because the more artificial an object is, the more true it is. The bowl of cherries on the kitchen table seems real enough, but in the theatre it just seems fake. In the theatre, when you design your own cherries, your own bowl and the table with great accuracy of expression, all this artifice contributes to the realness of what you have created. If I film the real sea, it'll look false. Try filming a plastic sea of your own invention and this created reality will be more interesting because it is an intensified reality, imbued with the power of suggestion.'

Amarcord, directed by Federico Fellini, 1973. Photo: Franco Pinna

Blade Runner, directed by Ridley Scott, 1982. Photo: Warner Brothers

The Day After Tomorrow, directed by Roland Emmerich, 2004. Photo: 20th Century Fox

Mission to Mars, directed by Brian De Palma, 2000. Photo: Walt Disney Co.

2012, directed by Roland Emmerich, 2009. Photo: Sony Pictures

Overleaf: Nicole Kidman and Ewan McGregor in *Moulin Rouge!*, directed by Baz Luhrmann, 2001.
Photo: 20th Century Fox

THAT'S ENTERTAINMENT

Strangers used to gather together at the cinema and sit together in the dark, like Ancient Greeks participating in the mysteries, dreaming the same dream in unison.

Angela Carter

Grauman's Chinese Theatre on Hollywood Boulevard. Photo: Richard Cummins

Cars at a drive-in, St. Louis, Missouri, 1946.
Photo: Car Culture

The time when screenings were held in basement cellars or in marquees at county fairs has long since passed.

The first 'cinema', for which, on 28 December 1895, an entrance fee was charged for the very first time, was in the basement bar of the Grand Café in Paris. And when this 'invention without a future' began to attract attention, the curious had to seek it out at county fairs, in between merry-go-rounds and exotic attractions, hidden amongst hoards of other booths. This early cinema was a child of vaudeville, curtain raisers and magic shows, and so it had to find its place in a space crowded with acrobats, conjurers and skimpily clad dancing girls; in a circus tent, no less.

It took the First World War and the shifting of the cinematic balance of power from Europe to America, on whose territory there was no fighting, to change the appearance of cinemas and to transform them into true cathedrals of entertainment. This metamorphosis meant that films changed from being comics, which lasted for one or two reels, to become spectacular creations that could last for two hours or more. The film industry was blossoming into full maturity, and in a few short years the first studios appeared in the hills of Hollywood. Meanwhile the European market began to rebuild itself. Above all, there was a public to please, one which was looking for longer lasting, more elaborate and more exciting entertainment.

A film needed to be shown in the right atmosphere, one which was just as magnificent, just as ambitious, just as opulent as itself. If films showed off their stars, why couldn't a cinema do the same, and adapt itself to the new scale of entertainment? This was at a time when ticket prices were being raised too: producers wanted better returns on their considerable investments and the cinema owners complied. From five cents the price went up to a dollar, and, in some cases, even higher. And so what was on offer at the cinema had to be appropriate: no more wooden benches, informal screens, or wobbly walls.

There was a whole range of establishments ready to satisfy every demand and every audience, from those who want to be seen at premieres to those who prefer the seclusion of the balcony seats, where they can find the peace (and intimacy) that they are denied elsewhere. In this way, the cinema as a place became inseparable from the cinema

A multiplex in St. Charles, Illinois, 2008.
Photo: Joshua Lutz

The Cathay Cinema, Shanghai, 2006.
Photo: Primo Yuan

George Clooney and Frances McDormand in
Burn After Reading, directed by Ethan and Joel Coen,
2008. Photo: Focus Features

as entertainment. Tangible proof of this can be found in the screens themselves, which had to keep on expanding to match the ambitions of the film-makers.

Then television put an end to these cathedrals of show business. Cinemas began to go into decline, and to resemble the ticket ladies, who were no longer as young as they used to be, and whiled away the time between one show and another by knitting. It seemed like an irretrievable loss. Until, that is, the time came when new cathedrals began to rise in the outskirts of cities. They were less enchanting, but even more gigantic; less elegant from an architectural point of view, but certainly more practical in terms of exploiting the attraction of cinema. And so began the era of the multiple screen cinemas, of multiplexes, of megaplexes: with five, eight, ten, even fifteen screens or more. Comfortable seats, gigantic screens, varied programmes. In some ways it's like a return to the golden age, but some of the romance of the cinema as a destination has certainly been lost forever.

P.M.

On 26 November 1952, the Paramount Theatre in Hollywood held the premiere of *Bwana Devil*, an adventure film in **3D**. The promotional ads for the film boasted 'The miracle of the age! A lion in your lap! A lover in your arms!' 3D was hailed as a revolution, one that could change the way that films were made, and potentially solve the crisis provoked by falling box-office returns. Virtually the same thing is happening all over again today: it is a case of *deja vu* for an entertainment industry that has to pull a rabbit out of the hat at regular intervals.

Bwana Devil was certainly not the first ever 3D film; that title goes to a film from 1922, *The Power of Love*. It is true, however, that *Bwana Devil* heralded a short-lived boom for 3D cinema between 1952 and 1954. The advent of television had caused a huge drop in cinema audience numbers and the production companies were in dire need of something spectacular to draw people back to movie theatres. 3D was, and remains, the perfect ploy; it holds the promise of a thrilling new visual experience, and yet it is also paradoxically a return to some of the very earliest days of cinema.

Bwana Devil had a run of almost three and a half months, a record for the period, but after this initial success, interest in 3D films faded away, not to be revived again until the 1980s and 90s.

The audience watching a 3D movie at the Paramount Theatre, Hollywood, 1952. Photo: J.R. Eyerman

Children at the cinema, 1958. Photo: Wayne Miller

Outside a cinema in Trastevere, Rome, 1953. Photo: Herbert List

450

A queue outside a cinema in
Manchester, waiting to see *Rock
Around the Clock*, directed by
Fred F. Sears, 1956.
Photo: Express Newspapers

Physicist Albert Einstein visits the set of the film *The Big House*, directed by George W. Hill, 1931.
Photo: Clarence Sinclair Bull

Soviet leader Nikita Khrushchev with Shirley MacLaine on the set of *Can-Can*, directed by Walter Lang, 1959.
Photo: Bob Henriques

In 2008, tourists visit the village outside Nefta, in southern Tunisia, where scenes from the first *Star Wars* movie were shot in 1977. Photo: Patrick Zachmann

Matamata in New Zealand, where the Hobbit village was built for the *Lord of the Rings* trilogy, is now a tourist attraction, 2004. Photo: Otto Pohl

Overleaf: Charlton Heston on-screen at an American drive-in showing *The Ten Commandments*, directed by Cecil B. DeMille, 1958. Photo: J.R. Eyerman

The Herbst Theatre in San Francisco, 1985. Photo: Rick Doyle

The historic La Pagode cinema, built in Paris in 1895 by Alexandre Marcel, 1993. Photo: Tatiana Markow

The Olimpia Cinema, Turin, 2003. Photo: Alessandro Albert and Paolo Verzone

The Doria Cinema, Turin, 2003. Photo: Alessandro Albert and Paolo Verzone

Overleaf: The audience watches a film being shown by a mobile cinema, Maharashtra, India, 2010.
Photo: Amit Madheshiya

Photographers on the red carpet at the Cannes Festival, 2001. Photo: Yves Herman

Previous pages: The foyer of the Warner Village multiplex, Milan, 2008. Photo: Massimo Siragusa

SOURCES OF ILLUSTRATIONS

p. 6 Eve Arnold/Magnum Photos
p. 10 Bruce Davidson/Magnum Photos
p. 12 Fabio Lovino/Contrasto
p. 13 Left to right: Everett Collection;
Scotty Welbourne/Eyevine; Columbia Pictures/
Courtesy Everett Collection
p. 14 Francesco Carrozzini/Trunk Archive
p. 15 Philippe Halsman/Magnum Photos
p. 17 Fabio Lovino/Contrasto
p. 18 Ernest Bachrach/Courtesy Everett Collection
p. 19 Courtesy Everett Collection
p. 21 Clarence Sinclair Bull/John Kobal Foundation/
Getty Images
p. 22 John Kobal Foundation/Getty Images
p. 23 William Walling Jr./John Kobal Foundation/Getty
Images
p. 25 Robert Coburn/Everett Collection
p. 27 Eugene Robert Richee/John Kobal Foundation/
Getty Images
p. 28 Philippe Halsman/Magnum Photos
p. 29 Album
p. 31 Philippe Halsman/Magnum Photos
p. 32 Album
p. 33 Album
p. 35 Philippe Halsman/Magnum Photos
p. 36 Paola Kudacki/Trunk Archive
p. 37 Michel Comte/Andreas Putsch Photo Collection
p. 38 David Hurn/Magnum Photos
p. 39 David Hurn/Magnum Photos
p. 40 Paul Ronald/Archivio Storico del Cinema/AFE
p. 41 Paul Ronald/Archivio Storico del Cinema/AFE
p. 43 Phil Stern/CPI
p. 44 George Hurrell/Courtesy Everett Collection
p. 45 George Fitzmaurice/GBB Archive/Contrasto
p. 46 Serge Cohen/Cosmos
p. 47 Henri Cartier-Bresson/Magnum Photos

p. 49 Philippe Halsman/Magnum Photos
p. 50 Henry Leutwyler/Contour/Getty Images
p. 51 Marco Grob /Trunk Archive
p. 52–53 Paolo Pellegrin/Magnum Photos
p. 54 Raymond Meier/Trunk Archive
p. 55 Martin Schoeller/August
p. 57 Fabio Lovino/Contrasto
p. 58 Gino Sprio/Eyevine
p. 59 Bruce Davidson/Magnum Photos
p. 60–61 Raymond Depardon/Magnum Photos
p. 63 Philippe Halsman/Magnum Photos
p. 64–65 Fabio Lovino/Contrasto
p. 66 Martin Schoeller/August
p. 67 Martin Schoeller/August
p. 69 Martin Schoeller/August
p. 70 Ladd Company/Warner Brothers/Album
p. 72 20th Century Fox Film Corp./Courtesy
Everett Collection
p. 73 Left to right: Everett Collection; Columbia Pictures/
Courtesy Everett Collection
p. 74–75 Everett Collection
p. 76 Warner Brothers/Courtesy Everett Collection
p. 77 Courtesy Everett Collection
p. 78 Universal/Courtesy Everett Collection
p. 79 Universal/Courtesy Everett Collection
p. 80 Columbia Pictures/Courtesy Everett Collection
p. 81 Everett Collection
p. 82–83 A. Palma Archive/Contrasto
p. 84 GBG Archive/Contrasto
p. 85 Pierluigi Praturlon/Reporters Associati
p. 86–87 Everett Collection
p. 88 Touchstone/Courtesy Everett Collection
p. 89 Everett Collection
p. 90–91 20th Century Fox Film Corp./Courtesy Everett
Collection
p. 92–93 Everett Collection

p. 215 Greg Williams/August
p. 216–17 Angelo Turetta/Contrasto
p. 218 David Hurn/Magnum Photos
p. 219 Susan Meiselas/Magnum Photos
p. 221 Album
p. 222–23 Douglas Kirkland/Corbis
p. 224 Phil Stern/CPI
p. 225 Everett Collection
p. 226–27 Angelo Turetta/Contrasto
p. 229 W. Eugene Smith/Magnum Photos
p. 230 Everett Collection
p. 232 20th Century Fox Film Corp./Courtesy Everett Collection
p. 233 Above left: 20th Century Fox Film Corp./Courtesy Everett Collection; above right: Everett Collection; below left: Everett Collection; below right: Lucasfilm Ltd/Courtesy Everett Collection
p. 234 Wilson Webb/Paramount Pictures/Courtesy Everett Collection
p. 236 Philippe Halsman/Magnum Photos
p. 237 David Hurn/Magnum Photos
p. 238 Above left: Everett Collection; above right: John Kobal Foundation/Getty Images; below left: Everett Collection; below right: John Kobal Foundation/Getty Images
p. 239 David Seymour/Magnum Photos
p. 240–41 Everett Collection
p. 242 Above left: Walt Disney Co./Courtesy Everett Collection; above right: 20th Century Fox Film Corp./Courtesy Everett Collection; below left: Everett Collection; below right: Album
p. 243 Album
p. 244–45 Everett Collection
p. 246 Eyevine
p. 248 Above right: Album; others on page: Everett Collection
p. 249 Below left: Everett Collection; others on page: Album
p. 250 Above left: Columbia Pictures/Courtesy Everett Collection; above right: 20th Century Fox/Courtesy Everett Collection; below left: Universal/Courtesy Everett Collection; below right: Buena Vista/Courtesy Everett Collection
p. 251 Philippe Halsman/Magnum Photos
p. 252–53 Everett Collection
p. 254 Orion Pictures/Album
p. 256 New Line Cinema/Album
p. 257 DreamWorks/Album
p. 258 Warner Brothers/Courtesy Everett Collection

p. 259 Album
p. 260 David Strick/Redux
p. 261 Below left: Clarence Sinclair Bull/Everett Collection; others on page: Everett Collection
p. 262 John Kobal Foundation/Getty Images
p. 263 20th Century Fox Film Corp./Courtesy Everett Collection
p. 264 Everett Collection
p. 266 Columbia Pictures/Courtesy Everett Collection
p. 267 Warner Brothers/Courtesy Everett Collection
p. 268 Everett Collection
p. 269 Album
p. 270 Everett Collection
p. 271 Jaap Bultendijk/Paramount Pictures/Courtesy Everett Collection
p. 272 Warner Brothers/Courtesy Everett Collection
p. 274 Above right: Dennis Stock/Magnum Photos; others on page: Everett Collection
p. 275 Eyevine
p. 276 Everett Collection
p. 277 John Kobal Foundation/Getty Images
p. 278 Above left: 20th Century Fox/Courtesy Everett Collection; above right: Orion Pictures Corp./Courtesy Everett Collection; below left: DreamWorks/Courtesy Everett Collection; below right: Avco Embassy/Album
p. 279 Miramax/Courtesy Everett Collection
p. 280–81 Douglas Kirkland/Corbis
p. 282 Warner Brothers/Courtesy Everett Collection
p. 284 Sony Pictures/Courtesy Everett Collection
p. 285 Burt Glinn/Magnum Photos
p. 286 Everett Collection
p. 287 Universal/Courtesy Everett Collection
p. 288 Warner Brothers/Courtesy Everett Collection
p. 289 Above left: 20th Century Fox Film Corp./Courtesy Everett Collection; above right: 20th Century Fox Film Corp./Courtesy Everett Collection; below left: Warner Brothers/Courtesy Everett Collection; below right: New Line Cinema/Courtesy Everett Collection
p. 290 Miramax/Courtesy Everett Collection
p. 292 Courtesy Everett Collection
p. 293 Everett Collection
p. 294 Everett Collection
p. 295 Above left: John Kobal Foundation/Getty Images; others on page: Everett Collection
p. 296 Tristar Pictures/Courtesy Everett Collection
p. 297 De Laurentiis Group/Courtesy Everett Collection
p. 298 Above left: Universal/Courtesy Everett Collection; others on page: Everett Collection

p. 299 Sony Pictures/Courtesy Everett Collection
p. 300 Martin Schoeller/August
p. 302 John Kobal Foundation/Getty Images
p. 303 Above: Clarence Sinclair Bull/Getty Images; below: Everett Collection
p. 304 Above left and right: Philippe Halsman/Magnum Photos; below left: Album; below right: Archivio Storico del Cinema/AFE
p. 305 Below left: CBS Photo Archive/Getty Images; others on page: Everett Collection
p. 306 Above left: Paramount/Courtesy Everett Collection; above right: Album; below left: Album; below right: Universal/Courtesy Everett Collection
p. 307 Warner Brothers/Courtesy Everett Collection
p. 308 Philippe Halsman/Magnum Photos
p. 309 Philippe Halsman/Magnum Photos
p. 311 Richard Avedon
p. 312 Art Streiber/August
p. 314 Sheryl Nields/August
p. 315 Everett Collection
p. 317 George Hurrell/Album
p. 318 Bruce Davidson/Magnum Photos
p. 319 John Engstead/John Kobal Foundation/ Getty Images
p. 321 George Hurrell/Courtesy Everett Collection
p. 322–23 GBB Archive/Contrasto
p. 325 Everett Collection
p. 326 Pierluigi Praturlon
p. 327 Alfred Eisenstaedt/Time&Life Pictures/ Getty Images
p. 329 Michel Comte/Andreas Putsch Photo Collection
p. 330 Herb Ritts/Trunk Archive
p. 331 Herb Ritts/Trunk Archive
p. 333 Herb Ritts/Trunk Archive
p. 334–35 Elliott Erwitt/Magnum Photos
p. 337 Eve Arnold/Magnum Photos
p. 338 Just Jaeckin/Sygma/Corbis
p. 339 Philippe Halsman/Magnum Photos
p. 340 Eyevine
p. 341 MGM/Courtesy Everett Collection
p. 342 Everett Collection
p. 343 Columbia Pictures/Courtesy Everett Collection
p. 345 Mario Tursi/Archivio Storico del Cinema/AFE
p. 346–47 Augusto Di Giovanni/Reporters Associati
p. 348 Jean Gaumy/Magnum Photos
p. 349 Serge Cohen/Cosmos
p. 350 Phil Stern/CPI
p. 352 Mark Peterson/Redux

p. 353 Left to right: Everett Collection; Vince Bucci/Getty Images
p. 355 Phil Stern/CPI
p. 356 Phil Stern/CPI
p. 357 Phil Stern/CPI
p. 358 Phil Stern/CPI
p. 359 Phil Stern/CPI
p. 361 William Klein
p. 362 Pierre Boulat/Cosmos
p. 363 Philippe Halsman/Magnum
p. 364 David Seymour/Magnum Photos
p. 365 Eve Arnold/Magnum Photos
p. 366 Bruce Davidson/Magnum Photos
p. 367 John Dominis/Time&Life Pictures/ Getty Images
p. 369 Dennis Stock/Magnum Photos/
p. 370 Yul Brynner/Trunk Archive
p. 371 Pierre Boulat/Cosmos
p. 372–73 Douglas Kirkland/Corbis
p. 374 Nicolas Tikhomiroff/Magnum Photos
p. 375 David Hurn/Magnum Photos
p. 377 Robert Capa © International Center of Photography/Magnum Photos
p. 378–79 Emanuele Scorcelletti/Contrasto
p. 380–81 Bruce Davidson/Magnum Photos
p. 382 Harry Gruyaert/Magnum Photos
p. 383 Martin Schoeller/August
p. 385 Paolo Pellegrin/Magnum Photos
p. 386 Paolo Pellegrin/Magnum Photos
p. 387 Martin Schoeller/August
p. 388 Art Streiber/August
p. 390 John Kobal Foundation/Getty Images
p. 391 Above left: Emanuele Scorcelletti/ Contrasto; above right: Davide Lanzilao/Contrasto; centre right: Denis Allard/Rea
p. 393 Elliott Erwitt/Magnum Photos
p. 394–95 Everett Collection
p. 397 Giancolombo/Contrasto
p. 398–99 Clarence Sinclair Bull/John Kobal Foundation/Getty Images
p. 400 Giancolombo/Contrasto
p. 401 Giancolombo/Contrasto
p. 403 Elio Sorci/David Secchiaroli Archive/Photomovie
p. 404 Below right: Mike Blake/Reuters; others on page: Gary Hershorn/Reuters
p. 405 Above left: Timothy A. Clary/AFP/Getty Images; others on page: Gary Hershorn/Reuters
p. 406–07 Art Streiber/August
p. 408 Eric Gaillard/Reuters

Memorabilia on sale in a shop on 34th Street, New York, 1993. Photo: Bruce Gilden

INDEX

of individuals named in photographs and captions